Mediterranean Diet

77 Delicious Recipes with an Easy Guide for Rapid Weight Loss and The Mediterranean Diet Cookbook with Delicious Recipes for Weight Loss

Book 1: Mediterranean Diet

77 Delicious Recipes with an Easy Guide for Rapid Weight Loss

Contents

Introduction

I want to thank you and commend you for opening the book, "Mediterranean Diet: 77 Delicious Recipes with an Easy Guide for Rapid Weight Loss".

This book contains easy, simple recipes that incorporate staples of the Mediterranean diet. These recipes include lots of fresh ingredients that contain antioxidants, minerals, vitamins, healthy fats and lean proteins that all promote health. These ingredients help reset your body and speed up your metabolism to burn excess fats. Weight loss is not about starving yourself and sweating for hours in the gym. Weight loss with the Mediterranean diet is all about enjoying good, fresh foods.

Thanks again for reading this book, I hope you enjoy it!

Creamy Panini

This is a healthy meal you can have for lunch or dinner that will keep you full longer and stave off unhealthy cravings.

Ingredients:
(Good for 4 sandwiches)
- 8 slices (about 1/2-inch thick) of rustic bread made with whole grain
- 1/2 cup mayonnaise dressing made with olive oil
- 2 tablespoons oil-cured black olives, finely chopped
- 1/4 cup fresh basil leaves, chopped
- 1 small zucchini, sliced thinly
- 1 7-oz. jar of roasted red peppers, liquid drained, sliced into large chunks
- 4 slices of provolone cheese

How to make:
- Place mayonnaise in a small bowl. Add olives and basil. Stir with a spoon until evenly combined. Divide the mayonnaise among the 8 slices of bread.
- Place 4 bread slices on a plate.
- Spread 1 side of a bread slice with mayonnaise.
- Top the bread (with mayo mix) with bacon, peppers, zucchini and 1 slice of provolone cheese. Top with another slice of bread.
- Spread the remainder of the mayonnaise mix outside the sandwiches.
- Toast both sides of the bread until golden and the cheese melts.

Mediterranean Pasta Salad

This is a great salad to add to your weight loss Mediterranean diet plan. It has resistant starch (natural fiber) that helps you burn about 25% more calories each day. This salad is also filling, which can keep you feeling full longer.

Ingredients:
(Good for 4 servings)
- 8 ounces of cooked multigrain farfalle (cooked without added salt and fat)
- 2 teaspoons of extra-virgin olive oil
- Zest and juice from 1 medium-sized lemon
- 1 13.5-ounce can of artichoke hearts packed in water, liquid drained and hearts chopped

- 1/4 cup chopped roasted red bell pepper
- 8 ounces of fresh part-skim mozzarella cheese, sliced into bite-sized cubes
- 1/2 cup of cooked peas
- 1/4 cup fresh parsley, roughly chopped

How to make:
- In a large bowl, mix olive oil, lemon zest and lemon juice.
- Toss in cheese, parsley, artichoke hearts, peas, pasta and bell pepper.
- Serve warm.

Mediterranean Tuna Salad

You can always enjoy rich tuna salad without worrying about getting too many calories in just 1 serving. The bold flavors of Mediterranean staples like olives, scallions and capers create a nice and satisfying combination.

Ingredients:
(Good for 6 sandwiches)
- 6 slices of whole wheat bread
- 2 6-oz. cans of tuna, liquid drained and tuna flesh flaked with a fork
- 1/4 cup pitted ripe olives, roughly chopped
- 1/4 cup mayonnaise dressing with olive oil
- 1/4 cup roasted red peppers, roughly chopped
- 1 tablespoon of small capers, liquid drained and then capers rinsed
- 2 green onions, sliced

How to make:
- Mix all the ingredients (except the slices of bread) in a medium-sized bowl.

- If desired, place a layer of greens (e.g., lettuce leaves, arugula, kale, etc.) on the bread slices before placing about a tablespoon or two of the tuna salad.
- Top with another slice of bread and enjoy.

Mediterranean Skewers with Bloody Mary Vinaigrette

This can be an appetizer or a healthy Mediterranean snack. The skewers are so easy to make. You can make the vinaigrette in a flash, and produce this healthy and delicious dish in an instant.

Ingredients:
(Good for 32 servings/skewers, with 1 ½ teaspoons of vinaigrette)
- About 32 pieces each of grape tomatoes, Bocconcini, Kalamata olives, and artichoke hearts
- 1/2 cup of tomato juice
- 1/8 teaspoon of Worcestershire sauce
- 2 tablespoons of premium vodka
- 2 celery hearts, finely minced, yields about 3 tablespoons
- 1/4 teaspoon black pepper, freshly ground
- 1/4 teaspoon salt
- 1/8 teaspoon of hot sauce
- 2 tablespoons of extra-virgin olive oil

- 1/4 teaspoon of prepared horseradish

How to make:
- Place hot sauce, tomato juice, Worcestershire sauce, celery, horseradish, olive oil and vodka in a bowl. Whisk together until smooth and evenly blended. Season with some pepper and salt. Set aside in the refrigerator.
- Thread Bocconcini ball, artichoke, olive and tomato in metal skewers. Serve with the vinaigrette.

Mediterranean-Style Detox Salad

This is a super-packed salad that can help with your detox. When you want to lose weight, you have to detox. Toxins in your body will promote the accumulation of more fats. These will also prevent you from losing as much weight as you want. Detox today with this wonderful and easy-to-do salad recipe.

Ingredients:
(Good for 4 servings, each serving is about 1 /2 cups of salad)
- 1 (8-ounce) English cucumber
- 2 tablespoons extra-virgin olive oil
- 2 tablespoons fresh lemon juice
- Black pepper, to taste
- 1 (14-ounce) can artichoke hearts, drained and quartered
- 6 cups trimmed watercress

- 2 large celery stalks, sliced
- 1/2 cup feta cheese
- 1/2 cup sliced red onion

How to make:
- Slice the cucumber lengthwise in half. Then slice crosswise into smaller, ¼-inch thick pieces.
- Get ¾ of the sliced cucumbers and place in a food processor. Add lemon juice. Pulse until smooth.
- Slowly pour olive oil into the food processor while pulsing. Pour in a thin stream. Keep pulsing until smooth and evenly combined.
- Pour the dressing in a large mixing bowl. Season with black pepper.
- Add the remainder of the cucumber, red onion, celery, artichoke hearts and watercress. Toss to coat all the vegetables with the dressing.
- Top with crumbled or cubed feta cheese before serving.

Mediterranean Salmon

Salmon is one of the healthiest fishes you should eat at least 2 times per week. Wild salmon is better than farm-raised fishes. Salmon and other fatty fishes are rich sources of monounsaturated fats such as omega-3 fats. This reduces inflammation that promotes fat accumulation.

Ingredients:
(Good for 4 servings, each serving ha 1 fillet and ½ cup of vegetables)

- 4 skinless salmon fillets, 6 ounces each, about 1 inch in thickness
- 1/4 teaspoon of black pepper
- 1/4 teaspoon of salt
- Cooking spray
- 2 cups of cherry tomatoes, sliced in half
- 2 tablespoons of capers, do not drain the liquid
- 1/2 cup zucchini, chopped finely

- 1 can, about 2 ¼ ounces, sliced ripe olives, liquid drained
- 1 tablespoon of extra virgin olive oil

How to make:
- Heat the oven to 425 degrees. Lightly coat a shallow baking dish with cooking spray.
- Season both sides of the fish with pepper and salt. Place on prepared baking dish.
- Mix the rest of the ingredients in a medium bowl. Spoon over the fillet.
- Bake salmon in the oven for 22 minutes, until the flesh easily flakes when a fork is inserted.

Greek-Style Picnic Salad

This is way better and healthier than regular pasta. Each serving is less than 300 calories, with 4 grams of fiber. You need more fiber in your diet to keep you full and keep cravings at bay.

Ingredients:
(Good for 10 servings, each serving is 1 cup of the salad)
- 2 cups of cooked white rice
- 1 1/2 tablespoons of extra virgin olive oil, divided
- 3/4 cup of sun-dried tomatoes, without oil
- 1 can (15 ½ ounces) garbanzo beans, liquid drained and rinsed
- 8 cups of fresh spinach leaves
- 2 cloves of garlic, minced
- 1/4 cup pitted Kalamata olives, coarsely chopped
- 1/2 teaspoon of salt
- 1 teaspoon of dried oregano
- 1/2 teaspoon black pepper, freshly ground
- 3 tablespoons toasted pine nuts
- 2 cups crumbled reduced-fat feta cheese

How to make:

- Soak sun-dried tomatoes in hot water until soft, about 30 minutes. Drain then slice into 1-inch bits.
- Sauté garlic and spinach in oil until spinach wilts, about 3 minutes. Transfer into a bowl.
- Add rice, cheese, tomatoes, garbanzo beans, oregano, black pepper and olives to the spinach. Drizzle with some olive oil and gently toss everything to coat.
- Spoon on a plate and sprinkle with pine nuts

Mediterranean Stuffed Tomatoes

Tomatoes are rich in lycopene that helps protect against cancer. This is also a great antioxidant that can get rid of toxins from your body. Free radicals and other toxins can help pack in the pounds. Remove toxins and free radicals to reduce weight.

Ingredients:
(Good for 4 servings, each serving is half of a tomato, stuffed)
- 2 large tomatoes
- 1/4 cup of crumbled goat cheese
- 1/2 cup garlic croutons
- 1/4 cup pitted Kalamata olives, sliced

- 2 tablespoons fresh basil or thyme, chopped
- 2 tablespoons of reduced-fat Italian salad dressing or vinaigrette

How to make:
- Preheat the broiler.
- Slice the tomatoes in half and remove seeds. Scoop out the pulp and coarsely chop. Add goat cheese, basil (or thyme), olives, dressing and croutons. Mix well.
- Place the hollow tomato shells on a paper towel, cut side down. Set aside to drain for 5 minutes.
- Spoon the filling inside the tomatoes.
- Arrange the filled tomatoes on a pan. Broil for 5 minutes until the cheese melts.

Warm Olives with Rosemary

This is a classic Mediterranean recipe. It is simple yet delicious. This is another great way to add more olives into your diet, with only 110 calories per serving. Snack on these or add as side dish.

Ingredients:
(Good for 1 cup, serving size is 2 tablespoons)
- 1 cup of black olives
- 1 cup of green olives
- 1/4 cup extra virgin olive oil
- 1/4 teaspoon of fennel seeds
- 1 sprig of rosemary
- 1 pinch of crushed red pepper

How to make:
- Simply place all the ingredients in a skillet. Heat over medium heat settings. Toss until the olives start to brown. Transfer to a serving plate and enjoy warm.

Mediterranean Breakfast Couscous

This is a power-packed breakfast that is high in proteins and fiber but low in calories. This will help keep you full and energized for the rest of the morning.

Ingredients:
(Good for 4 servings, each serving is 1 cup of couscous with 1 teaspoon of butter and 1/2 teaspoon sugar)
- 1 cup whole-wheat couscous, uncooked
- 3 cups of 1% low-fat milk

- 4 teaspoons of melted butter, divided
- 1 cinnamon stick, about 2 inches long
- 1/4 teaspoon of salt
- 1/4 cup of dried currants
- 1/2 cup of dried apricots, coarsely chopped
- 6 teaspoons of dark brown sugar, divided

How to make:
- Heat milk and cinnamon stick in a saucepan over medium-high setting until small bubbles appear around the edges. Do not allow the milk to boil. Remove the saucepan from heat.
- Add apricots, couscous, salt, currants and 4 teaspoons of brown sugar. Stir well and cover. Set aside for 15 minutes for the milk to seep into the ingredients.
- Remove the cinnamon stick.
- Scoop the couscous into 4 serving bowls and top with 1 teaspoon of melted butter and ½ teaspoon of brown sugar.

Mediterranean Pizza

This is a much healthier version of the take-out pizza. You can still enjoy your favorite foods while trying to lose weight, as long as you make healthy substitutions. For this recipe, you only get 290 calories from 2 slices!

Ingredients:
(Good for 4 servings, each serving is 1/4 of the pizza)
- 1 12-inch pre-made or prepared pizza crust
- 1/4 teaspoon of dried Italian seasoning
- 1/4 teaspoon of crushed red pepper
- 1 cup of crumbled goat cheese
- 6 pieces of pitted Kalamata olives, coarsely chopped
- 3 pieces of plum tomatoes, sliced into 1/4-inch thick pieces
- 1 can (14-ounce) of quartered artichoke hearts, liquid drained
- 1/4 cup chopped fresh basil leaves
- Cooking spray

How to make:
- Heat the oven to 450 degrees.
- Put dried Italian seasoning and red pepper on the pizza crust.

- Sprinkle the cheese on the crust.
- Arrange olives, artichoke hearts and plum tomatoes.
- Bake until the cheese is bubbly and the crust is crisp. Serve hot topped with chopped basil leaves.

Greek Salmon Burgers

This is another great recipe to get those omega-3s in your diet.

Ingredients:
(Good for 4 burgers)
- 1 pound of skinless salmon fillets, sliced into 2-inch bits
- Egg white from 1 large egg
- 1/2 cup of panko
- 1/4 teaspoon black pepper, freshly ground
- 1 pinch of salt
- 1/2 cup of sliced cucumber
- 4 toasted ciabatta rolls
- 1/4 cup of feta cheese, crumbled

How to make:
- Put salmon, egg white and panko in a food processor. Pulse until the fish is chopped finely.
- Form 4 patties from the fish mixture, each patty about 4 inches in diameter. Season each side with some pepper and salt.
- Grill the patties until done.
- Serve on a bed of greens or with a tablespoon of healthy dressing.

Roasted Red Peppers with Mediterranean Stuffing

Each serving is only 200 calories, with 3 grams of monounsaturated fats and 5 grams of fat. You also get loads of vitamins C from the bell peppers. This vitamin is a powerful antioxidant, which boosts immunity and protects your body against harmful free radicals. Vitamin K and A from spinach are antioxidants that help detoxify your body and help you lose weight faster.

Ingredients:

(Good for 6 servings, each serving is 1 stuffed pepper)

- 6 large red bell peppers
- 4 cloves of garlic, minced
- 1 tablespoon of olive oil
- 1 ½ cup of fresh spinach leaves
- 1 teaspoon of salt
- 1 tablespoon of freshly squeezed lemon juice
- 2 cups of cooked couscous
- 1/2 cup of crumbled feta cheese

How to make:

- Roast the bell peppers until the skins have blackened. Place in a re-sealable plastic bag and cool. Once cooled, peel the peppers. Cut off the stem and remove the seeds. Rinse and set aside.
- Sauté garlic in oil until golden brown. Add the spinach and cook until the leaves wilt. Transfer to a bowl. Add salt and lemon juice to the leaves.
- Toss in feta and cooked couscous.
- Stuff the bell peppers with the spinach-couscous filling. Bake for 8 minutes in a 350-degree preheated oven and serve hot.

Chicken Garbanzo Salad

This is another high fiber dish you should try and include in your weight loss diet. This is high in proteins and low in saturated fats, perfect for a filling but not fattening meal.

Ingredients:
(Good for 4 servings, each serving is 1 ¾ cup of salad)
- 1 9-oz. chicken breast, cut into small cubes
- 1 cup of cucumber, seeds removed and flesh chopped
- 1 15-oz. can of chickpeas, liquid drained and then rinsed
- 1/2 cup of chopped green onions
- 1/2 cup of plain fat-free yogurt

- 1/4 cup of chopped fresh leaves of basil or mint
- 1/4 teaspoon of salt
- 2 cloves of garlic, minced
- 2 cups of baby spinach leaves
- 1/3 cup crumbled feta cheese with cracked pepper
- 4 lemon wedges

How to make:
- Place all the ingredients, except feta cheese and spinach leaves, in a large bowl. Gently toss to mix everything well.
- Gently stir in the cheese and spinach leaves. Place in a serving dish and place lemon wedges.

Fluffy Pancakes

This is a healthy version of a breakfast favorite.

Ingredients:
(Good for 5 servings, each serving consists of 4 small pancakes)

- 1 large egg
- 1 1/2 cups Greek yogurt, low-fat variety
- 3/4 cup milk, fat-free
- 1 cup buckwheat or whole-wheat pancake mix
- (for serving)
- 2 tablespoons light maple syrup
- 1 cup fresh strawberries.
- 1 cup fat-free milk

How to make:

- Mix low fat Greek yogurt, egg, milk and pancake mix. Continue mixing until there are no lumps.
- Cook in a hot pan, forming small pancakes.
- Serve with a more Greek yogurt.

Mediterranean Sautéed Shrimp & Fennel

Shrimp is another healthy source of lean protein and omega-3s that can help you lose more weight while also building muscles.

Ingredients:
(Good for 4 servings)
- 1 tablespoon of extra virgin olive oil
- 1 pound raw shrimp, peeled and deveined
- 1 large fennel bulb, core removed and sliced into 2-inch strips
- 1 tablespoon of fresh oregano, chopped
- 1 15-ounce can diced tomatoes
- 1/4 teaspoon freshly ground pepper
- 2 tablespoons capers, rinsed
- 1/4 cup crumbled feta cheese

How to make:

- Sauté fennel in oil in a large skillet set over medium heat. Cook until fennel starts to brown. Add oregano and tomatoes. Cook for 3 seconds.
- Add shrimp and cook until pink.
- Stir in the pepper and capers.
- Mix well and serve with a sprinkle of feta.

Mediterranean Tuna Antipasto Salad

This easy to make salad makes a perfect snack or meal, with only a few calories but rich in omega-3 that reduces inflammation and improve fat metabolism.

Ingredients:
(Good for 4 servings)
- 2 6-oz. cans water-packed tuna chunk, drained and flaked
- 1 15-oz. can of beans
- 1 large red bell pepper, diced finely
- 1/2 cup of chopped fresh parsley leaves, divided
- 1/2 cup of red onion, finely chopped
- 4 teaspoons of capers, rinsed
- 1/2 cup of fresh lemon juice, divided
- 1 1/2 teaspoons of fresh rosemary, finely chopped
- 4 tablespoons of extra virgin olive oil, divided
- 1/4 teaspoon of salt
- Freshly ground pepper, to taste
- 8 cups of mixed salad greens

How to make:

- Mix onion, bell pepper, tuna, capers, parsley, 2 tablespoon of the oil, ¼ cup of the lemon juice, beans and rosemary in a medium-sized bowl. Season with some pepper.
- In a separate bowl, mix the remaining 2 tablespoons of oil, ¼ cup of lemon juice and salt. Add the salad greens and toss everything to mix.
- Divide and arrange the greens on 4 serving plates. Scoop a helping of the tuna salad over the greens. Serve.

Italian Egg-Drop Soup

This is a traditional light soup that is easy to do and low in calories.

Ingredients:
(Good for 6 servings, each serving is about 1 ½ cups)
- 1 1/3 cups whole-wheat small pasta shells
- 6 cups of chicken broth
- 4 large eggs, beaten lightly
- 2 cups of water
- 1 7-oz. can of chickpeas, rinsed
- 1 bunch of scallions, sliced with whites and greens divided
- 2 tablespoons of fresh lemon juice
- 3 cups of chopped fresh arugula
- 6 tablespoons of Parmesan cheese, freshly grated
- freshly ground pepper to taste
- pinch of freshly grated nutmeg

How to make:
- Place water, chickpeas, pasta, broth, nutmeg and scallion whites in a Dutch oven. Bring to a boil for 3 to 5 minutes, just before pasta shells are done.
- Add arugula and cook until it wilts. Reduce heat down to low setting.

- Stir constantly and slowly add the egg.
- Add pepper, lemon juice and green scallions.
- Scoop into bowls ad serve topped with Parmesan.

Tomato-&-Olive-Stuffed Portobello Caps

This makes an easy meal, which is also easy on the weight. The meaty flavor of the mushrooms can definitely replace unhealthy meats.

Ingredients:
(Good for 4 servings)

- 4 Portobello mushroom caps, stems and gills removed
- 1/4 cup Kalamata olives, chopped
- 2/3 cup plum tomatoes, chopped
- 2 teaspoons of extra virgin olive oil, divided
- 1 teaspoon garlic, minced
- 1/2 teaspoon of fresh rosemary, finely chopped
- 2 tablespoons of fresh lemon juice
- 1/8 teaspoon of fresh ground pepper

- 2 teaspoons of soy sauce

How to make:
- Heat the grill.
- Mix cheese, garlic, rosemary, tomatoes, olives, pepper and 1 teaspoon of oil.
- Mix lemon juice, soy sauce and remaining oil in a small bowl. Brush this all over the cleaned caps. Grill until soft.
- Fill the caps with the tomato-cheese mixture. Grill again until cheese melts. Serve hot.

Mediterranean Tuna-Spinach Salad

This makes a light dinner or lunch.

Ingredients:
(Good for 1 serving, each serving is 2 cups spinach, 1 cup tuna salad and 1 orange)
- 1 5-oz. can of tuna chunks packed in water, drained
- 1 1/2 tablespoons of tahini
- 1 1/2 tablespoons of water
- 1 1/2 tablespoons of fresh lemon juice
- 4 pitted Kalamata olives, chopped
- 2 tablespoons of parsley
- 2 tablespoons of crumbled feta cheese
- 1 medium orange, peeled and sliced
- 2 cups of baby spinach

How to make:
- Whisk water, tahini and lemon juice in a large bowl. Add parsley, feta, olives and tuna. Stir with a spoon to mix.
- Spoon the tuna mixture over 2 cups of spinach leaves. Serve with orange.

Roasted Halibut with Tangerine & Olive Tapenade

Here is another recipe to get you to eat more fish. You get lean proteins with the healthy omega-3s to keep your weight in check without starving yourself.

Ingredients:
(Good for 4 servings, each serving is a 4-oz. fish)

- 1 1/4 pounds of halibut, quartered
- 3-5 whole clementine or Pixie tangerines, divided
- 1 teaspoon of capers, rinsed and chopped
- 1/4 cup pitted green or Kalamata olives, chopped
- 1 teaspoon of fresh thyme, finely chopped

- 1 small clove of garlic, minced
- 1 tablespoon of extra virgin olive oil
- 1/2 teaspoon of ground pepper
- 1/2 teaspoon of salt

How to make:
- Heat oven to 400 degrees. Place parchment paper on a rimmed baking sheet.
- Get ½ teaspoon of zest from 1 clementine or tangerine and squeeze a tablespoon of the juice. Set aside.
- Mix thyme, zest, garlic, capers and olives. Add juice and oil.
- Slice the fruits into ¼-inch slices. Arrange into 4 beds on the lined baking sheet. Top the fruit beds with 1 fish with the skin side down. Sprinkle salt and pepper over the fish and top with 1 tablespoon of tapenade.
- Bake until thickest part of the fish easily flakes with a fork.

Scafata with Warm Fava Bean & Escarole Salad

This is a healthy spring-inspired meal you can enjoy sans the calories.

Ingredients:
(Good for 4 servings, each **serving is** about 3/4 cup of salad)
- 1 cup of fresh fava beans, shelled
- 4 cups of escarole, coarsely chopped
- 2 tablespoons of extra virgin olive oil
- 2 garlic cloves, minced
- 1 small onion, sliced
- 1/8 teaspoon of crushed red pepper, adjusted to taste
- 1 cup of peas
- 1/4 teaspoon ground pepper
- 1/2 teaspoon salt
- 1/4 cup packed chopped fresh basil and/or mint

How to make:
- Sauté garlic, crushed red pepper and onions in oil, in a large saucepan, until softened.
- Add peas, beans and escarole.
- Season with a small amount of pepper and salt.
- Stir until escarole wilts.

- Remove from the heat and add the herbs. Stir to mix and spoon into serving plates.

Mediterranean Fig Salad

This healthy, refreshing salad recipe contains only 11 grams of carb and 286 calories per serving.

Ingredients:
(Good for 2 servings)
- 1 cup of trimmed green beans, blanched
- 6 small figs, sliced into 4
- 1 shallot, sliced thinly
- 1 125-g mozzarella balls, torn into chunks
- ¼ cup of torn fresh basil
- 3 tablespoons of balsamic vinegar
- 1 tablespoon of fig jam
- 3 tablespoon of extra virgin olive oil

How to make:
- Toss beans, shallots, hazelnuts, basil, figs and mozzarella.
- Whisk fig jam, vinegar and olive oil. Pour over the salad and serve.

Spinach with Lemon Crumbs and Chili

Chili and lemon add a kick to this simple and low calorie, yet very filling salad.

Ingredients:
(Good for 2 servings)
- 2 tablespoon of butter
- 1/3 cup of breadcrumbs
- zest from 1 lemon
- 2 cloves of garlic, crushed
- 1 piece of red chili, sliced finely
- 2 cups of spinach leaves
- salt and pepper
-

How to make:

- Melt the butter and add breadcrumbs when butter starts to foam. Add chili, garlic and lemon zest.
- Stir and cook until the crumbs are crunchy and golden. Season with salt and pepper. Transfer to a plate and set aside.
- Place spinach to the same pan and cook until wilted. Season and place on a serving plate. Top with the crumbs and serve.

Mediterranean Cheese-Stuffed Baked Chicken

This is a cheesy dish, which is rich in lean proteins. Do not worry about the fat from the skin because the calories from it are balanced by other low-calorie ingredients. Each filling and satisfying serving contains 401 calories.

Ingredients:
(Good for 4 servings)
- 2 pieces of red bell pepper, seeded and sliced into chunks
- 1 red onion, sliced into wedges
- 2 teaspoon of olive oil
- 4 chicken breasts, skin on
- ¼ cup of herb & garlic soft cheese
- 1 cup of cherry tomatoes
- handful of pitted black olives
- salt and pepper

How to make:
- Preheat the oven to 200 degrees.
- Combine onion and pepper in a baking tray. Drizzle with half of the oil. Bake for 10 minutes.
- Insert a knife between the skin and the flesh of the chicken to make a pocket.

- Divide the cheese among the breasts and insert each portion into the pockets. Smooth the skin back to cover the cheese. Brush oil all over the chicken. Season with pepper and salt. Arrange on top of the baked pepper and onions.
- Sprinkle olives and tomatoes all over the chicken. Bake in the oven for 25-30 minutes until chicken is cooked through.

Roasted Peppers with Anchovies and Tomatoes

The vibrant colors are indicative of the rich antioxidant contents of the peppers. Add the healthy fats from the anchovies and more antioxidants from tomatoes and you get a power-packed dish.

Ingredients:
(Good for 2 servings)
- 4 pieces halved and seeded red peppers
- 1 50-g can of anchovies packed in oil, drained and halved
- 8 small tomatoes, sliced in half
- 2 cloves of garlic, slivered
- 2 sprigs of rosemary
- 2 tablespoons of olive oil

How to make:

- Toss peppers in a little oil and roast in a preheated 160C oven until soft, about 40 minutes.
- Place anchovies inside each pepper.
- Add garlic, rosemary and tomatoes. Drizzle olive oil and roast for another 30 minutes until tomatoes are soft.
- Cool to room temperature and serve.

Mussels with Chili & Tomatoes

Aside fatty fishes, mussels are also rich inomega-3s. This dish is also low in calorie, only 267, but full in flavor. It only has 11 grams but very filling.

Ingredients:
(Good for 4 servings)
- 1 kilogram (2.2 pounds) of fresh mussels
- 2 pieces of ripe tomatoes. diced
- 2 tablespoons of extra virgin olive oil
- 1 clove garlic, chopped finely
- 1 shallot, sliced thinly

- 1 green chili, seeds removed and sliced thinly
- ½ cup of dry white wine
- 1 teaspoon of tomato paste
- pinch of sugar
- handful of fresh basil leaves
- salt and pepper

How to make:
- Sauté shallot, chili and garlic in oil, in a large saucepan set over medium heat.
- Add wine and deglaze. Add paste, sugar and tomatoes. Season with some salt and pepper.
- Stir and simmer for 3 minutes.
- Add mussels and stir. Cover the saucepan tightly. Let the mussels cook in steam for 3 to 4 minutes. Uncover and discard any unopened shell. Serve topped with fresh basil leaves.

Baked Lemon Mussels

Here is another great recipe to let you enjoy the healthy goodness of mussels.

Ingredients:
(Good for 4 servings)
- 1 kilogram (2.2 pounds) of mussels, cleaned
- ¼ cup of toasted breadcrumbs
- Zest of 1 lemon
- ½ cup of butter
- 1 tablespoon of chopped parsley
- 1 tablespoon of minced garlic

How to make:
- Cook mussels for 2-3 minutes in boiling water. Discard any that remained closed. Cool slightly and remove one side of the shell.
- Heat the grill.
- Mix zest and breadcrumbs. Add parsley and garlic. Mix well.
- Place a small pat of butter on each mussel. Top with a small amount of the crumb mixture.
- Grill on high for 3-4 minutes.
- Serve hot.

Feta and Watermelon Fresh Salad with Crispbread

This refreshing salad can be a great snack to keep you energized and reduce your cravings when losing weight.

Ingredients:
(Good for 3 servings)
- 1 ½ kilograms (3.3 pounds) of watermelon, seeds removed and sliced into chunks
- ½ cup of cubed feta cheese
- handful of pitted black olives
- handful of flat leaf parsley, chopped
- handful of mint leaves, chopped
- 1 red onion, sliced into thin rings
- olive oil
- balsamic vinegar
- 3-4 pieces of crispbread

How to make:
- Toss watermelon with olives and feta cheese. Place on a serving plate. Sprinkle onion rings and herbs. Drizzle balsamic vinegar and olive oil.
- Serve with crispbread on the side. Use crispbread to scoop up the salad and eat.

Mediterranean Sardine Fresh Salad

Here is another sardine salad to try to get moreomega-3s into your diet. This is low in calories, yet very satisfying and filling. Each serving only has 140 calories - another excuse to eat more of this dish.

Ingredients:
(Good for 4 servings)
- 1 cup of mixed salad leaves
- handful of pitted black olives, chopped coarsely
- 1 tablespoon of capers
- 2 120-g cans of sardines in tomato sauce, drain and reserve sauce
- 1 tablespoon of olive oil
- 1 tablespoon of red wine vinegar

How to make:
- Divide salad leaves into 4, placing each in a serving plate.
- Sprinkle capers and olives into each plate. Roughly slice the sardines and top to each salad.
- Whisk reserved tomato sauce, vinegar and oil. Drizzle over the salads and serve.

Mediterranean Chunky Tomato Soup

Low calorie and easy to make, this soup is a perfect accompaniment to any meal or as a warming snack. Each serving only has 212 calories.

Ingredients:
(Good for 4 servings)
- 2 cups of grilled vegetable mix (onions, aubergines, peppers, courgettes)
- 2 tablespoon of minced garlic
- handful of fresh basil leaves
- 2 cups of chopped tomatoes
- 1/6 cup of ricotta cheese
- 2 cups of water

How to make:

- Sauté garlic and half of the vegetable mix in a large pan set over high heat until softened. Add tomatoes, water and basil. Bring to a simmer.
- Use a hand blender to blitz the soup until it turns smooth.
- Add the rest of the vegetable mix and cover the pan. Cook until the vegetables are tender, about 15-20 minutes. Scoop into bowls and top with ricotta.

Mediterranean Marinated Vegetables

Olive oil, garlic and herbs make a wonderful marinade that adds more flavor to vegetables. Each serving is only 212 calories, perfect when trying to keep calories down to lose weight,

Ingredients:
(Good for 4 servings)
- 1 full garlic head, peeled
- 2 tablespoon of fresh thyme
- 1 tablespoon of fresh rosemary
- 8 fresh bay leaves
- 1 tablespoon of salt
- 2-3 teaspoons of black peppercorns, cracked
- ½ cup of olive oil

- 2 to 3 pounds of assorted vegetables, such as courgettes, aubergines, sweet potatoes, asparagus, corn cobs, new potatoes, red onions and fennel.

How to make:
- Place garlic, rosemary, peppercorns, thyme, oil, salt and bay leaves in a food processor. Pulse until everything is well combined.
- Slice the vegetables into thick chunks roughly about the same size. Mix the vegetables and toss in the marinade. Allow to marinate for about 2 hours. Grill until tender.

Warm Prawn with Rice Salad

This is a quick and easy meal you can make in under 10minutes. Enjoy a 403-calorie serving with the goodness of lean proteins and omega-3 from prawns.

Ingredients:
(Good for 2 servings)
- 1 250-g pouch of Mediterranean tomato rice, cooked according to package direction
- 1 250-g pack of jumbo tiger prawns, cooked
- 1 large courgette, diced
- 1 teaspoon of fresh lemon juice
- handful of torn basil leaves
- 1 tablespoon of olive oil
- 1 60-g bag of mixed salad leaves
- Pepper and salt

How to make:
- Place cooked rice in a large bowl. Add cooked prawns, basil and courgette.
- Pour oil and lemon juice.
- Season to taste.
- Toss to mix and then scoop on serving plates. Drizzle with more olive oil and enjoy.

Burnt Orange & Escarole Salad

This healthy salad uses honey as a natural sweetener. By caramelizing it, it gives a different flavor dimension to the dish.

Ingredients:
(Good for 12 servings, each **serving is** about 1 cup
- 16 cups torn escarole
- 2 sprigs of fresh rosemary, chopped
- 1/3 cup of extra virgin olive oil
- 1/4 cup of honey
- 3 tablespoons of apple cider vinegar
- 2 tablespoons of shallot, minced
- 2 tablespoons of freshly squeezed orange juice
- 3 medium oranges, peeled then sliced crosswise into 4 thick slices
- 1/2 teaspoon of salt
- 1/3 cup toasted slivered almonds

How to make:
- Bring honey and rosemary to a boil in a small saucepan over medium heat. Remove from heat and allow mixture to steep for about 30 minutes.

- Strain to remove rosemary bits.
- Pour honey in a skillet and place over medium-high heat. Bring it to a boil then add the orange slices. Cook until the orange starts to brown. Turn the oranges and cook the other side. Remove the oranges and set aside.
- In a separate large bowl, whisk orange juice, vinegar, shallot, salt and oil.
- Pour caramelized honey into the dressing and whisk to mix everything well.
- Add escarole to the bowl and toss to coat. Serve topped with cooked orange slices and some almonds.

Edamame & Chicken Greek Salad

Edamame is an excellent source of protein without the healthy fats.

Ingredients:
(Good for 4 servings, each **serving is** 2 3/4 cups)
- 1 8-oz. chicken breast, boneless, skinless, trimmed
- 3 tablespoons of extra virgin olive oil
- 1/4 cup of red wine vinegar
- 1/4 teaspoon of salt
- 1 1/2 cups shelled edamame
- 1/4 teaspoon of ground pepper
- 8 cups of chopped romaine
- 1/2 of a large European cucumber, sliced
- 1 cup of halved grape or cherry tomatoes
- 1/2 cup feta cheese, crumbled

- 1/4 cup Kalamata olives, sliced
- 1/4 cup fresh basil leaves, sliced into thin strips
- 1/4 cup red onion, slivered

How to make:
- Cook chicken until well done. Transfer to a cooling rack. Once cooled, slice into bite-sized pieces.
- In a bowl, whisk oil and vinegar. Season with pepper and some salt. Add feta, cucumber, olives, chicken, onion tomatoes, romaine, basil and edamame. Gently toss to coat everything.

Pesto Chicken & Cannellini Bean Soup

This Italian-inspired dish is full of fiber with an extra flavor boost from pesto.

Ingredients:
(Good for 8 servings, each serving is 1 3/4 cups)
- 2 pounds of chicken breasts, skinless
- 8 cups of low-sodium chicken broth
- 2 tablespoons of extra virgin olive oil
- 2 large garlic cloves, minced
- 1 cup of sliced onion
- 1 tablespoon of chopped fresh marjoram
- 1 tablespoon of chopped fresh oregano

- 3 cups fennel, sliced
- 2 cups sliced tomatoes
- 3 cups broccolini, sliced into 1-inch pieces
- 1 15-oz. can of cannellini beans, drained and rinsed
- 1/2 teaspoon of ground pepper
- 1 1/4 teaspoons of salt
- 1/4 cup of prepared pesto

How to make:
- Sauté garlic and onions in oil, in a large pot, until softened. Add marjoram and oregano. Stir and cook for another minute.
- Add chicken and broth. Cover the pot and raise the heat to high until the broth starts to simmer. Reduce heat and cook until chicken is done. Remove chicken and cool. Shred the met and discard the bone.
- In the same pot, add tomatoes, fennel and broccolini. Allow the broth to simmer. Continue cooking until the vegetables become tender. Add the shredded chicken and beans. Season with a small amount of pepper and salt. Cook until beans and chicken have been heated through. Remove from the heat and add pesto.

Creamy Pesto Chicken Salad with Greens

This is a healthier version of the classic chicken salad. Half of the mayonnaise is replaced by pesto, making it creamy but still healthy. This is served with greens instead of white bread to reduce calories.

Ingredients:
(Good for 4 servings, each **serving is** 2 cups greens and 1/2 cup chicken salad)

- 1 pound cooked chicken breast, shredded
- 1/4 cup of low-fat mayonnaise
- 1/4 cup of pesto sauce
- 3 tablespoons of red onion, finely chopped
- 2 tablespoons of red-wine vinegar
- 2 tablespoons of extra virgin olive oil
- 1/4 teaspoon of salt

- 1 5-ounce package (about 8 cups) of mixed salad greens
- 1/4 teaspoon of ground pepper
- 1 ½ cups of cherry or grape tomatoes, sliced in half

How to make:
- Mix mayonnaise, onion and pesto in a medium-sized bowl. Add shredded chicken and toss to mix well.
- In a large bowl, whisk vinegar and oil. Season with some pepper and salt. Mix well. Add the tomatoes and greens. Toss to evenly coat the vegetables.
- Divide the green salad between 4 serving plates. Top with a spoonful or so of the chicken salad. Enjoy.

Marinated Olives with Feta Cheese

This is a low calorie snack or side dish you can enjoy. You can serve this on warm baguette slices or crisp flatbread crackers.

Ingredients:
(Good for 1 ½ cups)
- 1 cup pitted olives, such as Kalamata, sliced into smaller rings
- 1/2 cup feta cheese, diced
- 1 teaspoon coarsely chopped fresh rosemary
- 2 tablespoons of extra-virgin olive oil
- 2 cloves of garlic, roughly chopped

- Pinch of crushed red pepper, more if desired
- Zest and juice from 1 medium-sized lemon
- Freshly ground pepper, adjusted to taste

How to make:
- Simply mix everything in a bowl and spoon over whole wheat crackers, pita or baguette.

Mediterranean Picnic Snack

This is a perfect refreshing and energizing snack that does not pack a lot of calories.

Ingredients:
(Good for 1 serving)
- 1 slice of crusty whole-wheat bread, sliced into bite-size pieces
- 1/4 ounce slice of aged cheese
- 10 pieces of cherry tomatoes
- 6 pieces of oil-cured olives

How to make:
- Just arrange everything in a serving plate and enjoy.

Spiced Eggs

This is a simple dish that gives a good dose of proteins and fats. Have this for a filling snack or as a side dish.

Ingredients:
(Good for 1 serving)
- 1 hard-boiled egg, sliced
- ¼ teaspoon of paprika
- Salt, to taste
- 1 tablespoon of extra virgin olive oil

How to make:
- Dip the egg slices in olive oil.
- Sprinkle each side with paprika and salt.
- Enjoy.

Mediterranean Herbed Tomato Sandwich

This is another healthy and refreshing Mediterranean snack. You can enjoy this without having to worry about eating too many calories as this is a low-carbohydrate recipe.

Ingredients:
(Good for 4 servings)
- 4 slices of whole-wheat bread
- 4 thick slices of tomato
- 8 teaspoons of reduced-fat mayonnaise, divided
- 4 teaspoons of chopped fresh basil leaves
- 1/8 teaspoon of freshly ground pepper
- 1/8 teaspoon of salt

How to make:
- Slice in the breads in rounds, slightly larger than the tomato slices.
- Spread 2 teaspoons of mayonnaise over each bread.
- Place one tomato slice on each bread slice. Sprinkle with basil leaves and season with pepper and some salt.

Date Wraps

This is a tasty, sweet and savory recipe low in carbohydrates.

Ingredients:
(Good for 16 pieces)
- 16 whole pieces of pitted dates
- 16 thin slices of prosciutto
- Freshly ground pepper, adjusted to taste

How to make:

- Take a slice of prosciutto and carefully wrap it around one pitted date. Place on a plate and ground pepper on top. Serve and enjoy.

Blueberries with Lemon Cream

Who says you can't enjoy something sweet while trying to lose weight? Try this recipe. You can also substitute any fresh fruit for this recipe.

Ingredients:
(Good for 4 servings, each serving is ½ cup)

- 2 cups of fresh blueberries
- 4 ounces of cream cheese, reduced-fat variety
- 1 teaspoon of honey
- 3/4 cup low-fat vanilla yogurt
- 2 teaspoons of freshly lemon zest
- How to make:
- Break up the block of cream cheese with a fork.
- Drain excess liquid from the yogurt and place in a bowl, with the cream cheese.
- Add honey and beat at high speed using an electric mixer until creamy and light.
- Fold in the lemon zest.
- Chill.
- In a dessert glass, layer lemon cream and blueberries.

Tomato-Basil Skewers

This is a simple recipe but the flavors are amazing. It is low in calorie and carbohydrates but high in vitamins and minerals that help burn fats.

Ingredients:
(Good for 16 skewers)
- 16 small fresh mozzarella balls
- 16 cherry tomatoes
- 16 fresh basil leaves
- Coarse salt & freshly ground pepper, to taste
- Extra-virgin olive oil, to drizzle

How to make:
- Thread tomatoes, basil and cheese alternately on small metal or wooden skewers.
- Drizzle with olive oil.
- Season with salt and pepper.

Cherries with Ricotta & Toasted Almonds

This is a decadent, rich dessert or snack that is low in calories. This recipe is also low in saturated fats and sodium but high in fiber.

Ingredients:
(Good for 1 serving)
- 3/4 cup of pitted cherries
- 1 tablespoon of slivered almonds, toasted
- 2 tablespoons of part-skim ricotta

How to make:
- Warm the cherries in a microwave or skillet on medium low heat.
- Place the cherries in a serving bowl and top with the ricotta cheese and almonds.

Greek Marinated Chicken

This is a classic Mediterranean chicken recipe that is low in calories. You only get about 364 calories in each serving. It is filling yet not fattening.

Ingredients:
(Good for 8 servings)
- ½ cup of extra virgin olive oil
- 3 cloves of garlic, crushed
- 1 tablespoon of fresh rosemary, chopped
- 1 tablespoon of fresh thyme, chopped
- 1 tablespoon of fresh oregano, chopped
- Juice from 2 lemons

- 1 1800-g chicken, skin and bones removed then cut into smaller pieces

How to make:
- Mix the herbs, garlic, lemon juice and olive oil in a glass dish. Add the chicken pieces and mix. Cover the glass dish and marinate the chicken in the refrigerator for at least 8 hours or overnight.
- Heat a grill over high settings. Lightly oil the grate.
- Once the grill is hot, place the marinated chicken and grill for about 15 minutes per side. The chicken is done when the juices are clear.

Greek Beans

This is another classic dish that packs lots of healthy proteins and fiber. Per serving, this recipe only gives 275 calories.

Ingredients:
(Good for 8 servings)
- 2 cups of butter beans
- 1/8 cup of extra virgin olive oil
- 3 small onions, sliced
- 3 cloves of garlic, crushed
- 1 teaspoon of fresh thyme
- 1 tablespoon of fresh oregano
- 5 cups of fresh tomatoes, chopped
- 1 tablespoon of tomato puree
- 1 teaspoon of brown sugar

- 3 tablespoon of fresh parsley
- ¼ teaspoon of salt
- ¼ teaspoon of black pepper, freshly ground

How to make:
- Soak washed beans overnight in clean, cold water. Drain the next day, and rinse.
- Place the beans in a saucepan and cover with lots of cold water. Bring to a boil over high heat for 10 minutes.
- Lower the heat and simmer for 20 to 30 minutes, until lightly cooked (outside is still firm and the middle is slightly hard). Drain the beans and set aside.
- In the same saucepan, add olive oil and sauté the thyme, oregano, garlic and onions until pale golden in color. Add tomatoes. Pour about half a cup of water to help cook the tomatoes.
- Add half a cup of water to help cook the tomatoes. color. e is slightly hard) Sugar and tomato puree. Break up the tomatoes and stir. Season with pepper and salt.
- Cover the saucepan and simmer until the sauce thickens.

- Heat the oven to 350 degrees Fahrenheit.
- Once the sauce thickens, stir in the parsley. Add the beans and stir.
- Pour the bean mixture in a baking dish. Bake in the oven for 30 minutes.
- Remove from the oven and serve hot.

Greek Salad Topped with Sardines

Sardines are another omega-3 rich fish you should try. This recipe can get you to eat more sardines. This is low in calorie and high in calcium.

Ingredients:
(Good for 4 servings, 2 cups per serving)
- 3 tablespoons of fresh lemon juice
- 1 garlic clove, minced
- 2 tablespoons of extra virgin olive oil
- 2 teaspoons of dried oregano
- 3 medium tomatoes, sliced into large chunks
- 1/2 teaspoon of freshly ground pepper
- 1 large English cucumber, sliced into large chunks
- 1/3 cup feta cheese, crumbled
- 1 15-oz. can chickpeas, drained and rinsed
- 1/4 cup red onion, thinly sliced
- 2 4-oz. cans sardines with bones, packed in water or olive oil, drained
- 2 tablespoons of sliced Kalamata olives

How to make:

- Mix oil, lemon juice, pepper, garlic and oregano in a large bowl. Whisk until well combined.
- Add chickpeas, olives, onions, cucumber, tomatoes and feta. Toss gently to combine everything.
- Divide salad between 4 serving plates. Serve topped with sardines.

Greek Tuna Pomodoro

This healthy recipe lets you enjoy pasta without the guilt. It is low in cholesterol and sodium and high in fiber.

Ingredients:
(Good for 4 servings, each serving is ½ cup of the pasta)
- 8 ounces whole-wheat spaghetti
- 2 tablespoons extra-virgin olive oil
- 1 tablespoon minced garlic
- 2 anchovies, minced (optional)
- 1/4 teaspoon crushed red pepper, or to taste
- 1 28-ounce can diced tomatoes
- 1 6-ounce can chunk light tuna, drained and flaked (see Note)
- 2 tablespoons thinly sliced fresh basil

How to make:
- Cook spaghetti in boiling water according to package directions. Drain and set aside.
- Sauté garlic in oil, in a large skillet. Add red peppers and anchovies. Cook for another 30 seconds.

- Add tomatoes and reduce heat down to medium. Cook for 8 minutes, stirring occasionally. Add tuna and cook until heated through.
- Pour sauce over pasta. Serve warm.

Mediterranean Grilled Chicken

Low calorie, at 167 per serving but full of delicious goodness. Do not worry about the skin on. Grilling it will render the fat and will make the breast juicy and tender.

Ingredients:
(Good for 6 servings, each serving half of a chicken breast)
- 6 bone-in chicken breast halves
- 3 tablespoons Rosemary-Garlic Rub
- 6 thyme sprigs
- 6 rosemary sprigs

- 1/2 teaspoon freshly ground black pepper
- Cooking spray

How to make:
- Loosen the skin and rub the rosemary-garlic mix between the skin and meat. Insert 1 thyme and 1 rosemary sprig. Press the skin back into the flesh to secure the sprigs. Set aside in the refrigerator for 4 hours.
- Prepare the grill, and lightly coat with cooking spray.
- Season both sides of the chicken with pepper. Grill with the skin side down. Cook for 25 minutes until meat is cooked through. Once done, discard the skin. Serve hot with grilled vegetables like tomatoes and onions or over green salad.

Greek Power Breakfast

Breakfast should be packed with energy but it should still be low in calories. Try this simple and delicious recipe that has all the vitamins, antioxidants and minerals that will pump your metabolism all day.

Ingredients:
(Good for 1 serving)
- 1 cup of Greek yogurt, vanilla flavored or plain
- ½ cup of fresh or frozen blueberries
- ¼ cup of raspberries
- 1 mint sprig
- 1 tablespoon of toasted almonds
- How to make:
- Mix everything in a bowl and enjoy.

Mushroom Omelette with Spinach

Make this dish for breakfast or lunch and enjoy the fat-burning effects of the antioxidants in spinach.

Ingredients:
(Good for 1 serving)
- 1 teaspoon of olive oil, divided
- ½ cup of sliced wild mushrooms
- handful of spinach
- 1/8 cup of soft cheese, low fat version
- pinch of grated nutmeg
- 2 medium eggs

How to make:
- Sauté mushrooms in ½ teaspoon of oil. Add spinach and cook until wilted. Transfer to a plate and stir in nutmeg and cheese.

- In the same pan, heat the remaining oil and add the eggs. Once the edges start to set, scoop the spinach-mushroom mixture over the eggs. Fold half of the omelette over the vegetables and cook until done. Serve hot.

Mediterranean Tuna-Bean Salad

Beans are healthy protein and carbohydrate sources. This is also another staple in the Mediterranean diet.

Ingredients:
(Good for 1 serving)
- 1 red onion, diced
- juice from 1 lemon
- 1 teaspoon olive oil
- ¼ cup of cooked green beans, halved
- 1 teaspoon of capers
- 120 grams of canned mixed beans, drained
- 2 teaspoon of tomato puree
- 5 pieces of cherry tomatoes
- 1 cup of salad greens
- 1 56-g tin of tuna chunks in water
- fresh ground pepper

How to make:
- Mix onions, beans, juice, oil, capers, mixed beans, tomatoes and tomato puree in a bowl.
- Scoop over a bed of mixed salad greens.
- Top with tuna chunks.
- Sprinkle with freshly ground black pepper.

Mediterranean Breakfast Fruit Compote

This is a refreshing dish, packed with metabolism-boosting antioxidants, minerals and vitamins.

Ingredients:
(Good for 1 serving)
- 3 canned apricot halves
- 3 tablespoons of juice from canned apricot
- 3 prunes
- 1 pear, quartered
- pinch of cinnamon
- ½ cup of Greek yogurt
- 1 teaspoon of toasted pumpkin seeds

How to make:
- Place apricot, pears, prunes and reserved apricot juice in a small saucepan. Heat over medium-low setting. Once heated through, add a pinch of cinnamon and transfer to a bowl.
- Top with yogurt and a sprinkle of pumpkin seeds.

Couscous with Smoked Mackerel

Have this for lunch or dinner and get the inflammation-busting omega-3 from the fish to keep fats at bay.

Ingredients:
(Good for 1 serving)
- grated zest from ½ of an orange
- Juice from ½ of an orange
- ¼ cup of dry couscous
- 1 cucumber, sliced
- 1 spring onion, slivered
- 1 medium carrot, grated
- ¼ cup of smoked mackerel fillet, flaked
- boiling water
- handful of watercress

How to make:
- Mix couscous with orange zest and juice.
- Add enough boiling water to cover the couscous. Soak for about 10 minutes.
- Add cucumber, carrot, mackerel and spring onion to the couscous. Mix.
- Transfer to a serving plate and serve with watercress.

Oat and Apricot Breakfast Smoothie

This is an energizing breakfast perfect for busy days.

Ingredients:
(Good for 1 serving)
- 1 cup of skimmed milk
- 1 tablespoon of oats
- ½ cup of canned apricots, drained

How to make:
- Place everything in a blender and pulse until smooth and well combined.
- Pour in a glass and enjoy.

Mediterranean Baked Tomatoes and Eggs

Get healthy proteins and fats from eggs and your daily dose of powerful antioxidants from tomatoes.

Ingredients:
(Good for 4 serving)
- 1 kg (2.2 lbs) of fresh, ripe tomatoes
- 1 teaspoon of olive oil
- 1 tablespoon of dried oregano
- 4 eggs

How to make:
- Slice tomatoes in half and arrange tightly packed in a baking dish.

- Drizzle with oil and sprinkle oregano. Bake for 15 minutes in a hot oven until softened. Remove from the oven.
- Make 4 holes in between the tomatoes. Crack 1 egg in each hole.
- Return the baking dish in the oven and bake until eggs are set.
- Serve with ciabatta bread on the side.

Mediterranean Pasta with Prawns

Have your pasta with omega-3-rich prawns for a balanced meal. You get carbs from pasta, proteins and fats from prawns.

Ingredients:
(Good for 1 serving)
- ¼ cup of cooked farfalle pasta
- 2 tablespoons of Greek yogurt
- 1 tablespoon of chopped fresh dill
- 1 teaspoon of capers
- squeeze of lemon juice
- ¼ cup of cherry tomatoes, quartered
- 1 spring onion, chopped
- 80 grams of cooked prawns
- lemon zest
- 1 handful of watercress
- pepper and salt to taste

How to make:
- Make the dressing by mixing yogurt, dill, lemon juice and capers. Whisk well.
- Mix pasta and prawns. Toss in spring onions, watercress, lemon zest and cherry tomatoes. Season with a little salt and pepper.

- Pour the yogurt dressing over the pasta. Toss gently and serve.

Tortilla Pizza

Enjoy your pizza with tortilla as a healthier crust substitute.

Ingredients:
(Good for 2 servings)
- 1 large tortilla wrap
- 3 tablespoons of tomato puree
- 2 tablespoon of grated mozzarella
- 1 tomato, sliced
- 1 tablespoon of dried Italian herbs
- black pepper
- 3 pitted olives, sliced in half

How to make:
- Place the tortilla on a baking sheet.
- Spread tomato puree. Top with cheese, tomatoes and herbs.
- Season with fresh ground pepper and add olives. Bake in the hot oven until the tortilla becomes crisp. Serve hot.

Lamb Burger with Feta and Salsa

Enjoy a hearty burger with a better, healthier substitute for beef- lamb. It has good lean meat that packs a great flavor without all the fat.

Ingredients:
(Good for 1 patty)
- 100 grams of lean lamb meat, minced
- 1 garlic clove, crushed
- 1 teaspoon chopped fresh rosemary
- 2 tablespoons of feta cheese
- ½ teaspoon of dried oregano

Salsa
- 4 cherry tomatoes, quartered
- 1 spring onion, sliced
- 2 black olives, chopped
- 1 tablespoon of red wine vinegar
- 1 teaspoon olive oil
- 1 tablespoon chopped fresh parsley

How to make:
- Mix lamb, rosemary, feta, oregano and garlic. Form into a patty and grill until cooked through.

- Mix the ingredients for the salsa and scoop over the grilled patty. Serve immediately.

Smoked Haddock Florentine

Fish and more fish. That is classic Mediterranean meal.

Ingredients:
- 175 grams of smoked haddock fillet, skinless and poached
- 1 medium egg
- Large handful of spinach

How to make:
- Poach the egg. Set aside.
- Pour boiling water over the spinach leaves. Press with a spoon to remove excess water.
- Arrange the spinach leaves on a plate. Top with poached haddock and egg. Serve.

Minestrone

Have a bowl of warm soup to soothe your soul and relax the body. Stress is a main driving factor for fat accumulation. De-stress with this simple recipe.

Ingredients:
(Good for 1 serving)
- ½ teaspoon of olive oil
- 1 spring onion, slivered
- ½ courgette, chopped
- ½ cup green beans
- 1 ½ cup of vegetable broth
- 1 teaspoon of Italian herbs
- 30 grams of small pasta shells, uncooked
- 2 tablespoons of peas
- 2 teaspoon of pesto sauce

How to make:

- Sauté spring onion in oil. Add courgette and green beans. Cook for a few minutes.
- Add vegetable stock and Italian herbs.
- Bring to a boil then reduce heat to a simmer. Cook for 2 minutes.
- Add pasta and cook until almost done. Add peas. Simmer for 2 minutes.
- Pour in a serving bowl and stir in the pesto.

Fillet steak with Mediterranean Vegetable Medley

Fish and vegetables give a filling and energizing meal anytime of the day.

Ingredients:
(Good for 1 serving)
- 1 courgette, sliced
- 1 red pepper, sliced
- 4 asparagus spears
- 1 teaspoon olive oil
- 1 teaspoon of balsamic vinegar
- 1 teaspoon chopped rosemary leaves
- 150 grams of lean fillet steak
- ½ cup of cherry tomatoes

How to make:
- Toss courgette, asparagus and red pepper in ½ teaspoon oil and balsamic vinegar. Grill until tender.
- Brush the remaining oil all over the fillet steak. Rub chopped rosemary and grill until done.
- Serve the grilled steak along with grilled vegetables, topped with fresh cherry tomatoes.

Creamy Pesto Mediterranean Chicken

Try this creamy chicken recipe with only a few calories per serving.

Ingredients:
(Good for 1 serving)
- 165 grams of chicken breast, skinless and boneless
- 1 teaspoon of olive oil
- ½ cup of chopped cherry tomatoes
- 1 tablespoon of crème fraiche
- 1 tablespoon of pesto
- Juice from 1 lemon
- Fresh basil leaves

How to make:
- Pan fry the chicken breast in olive oil until golden and cooked through.
- Add the tomatoes in the pan and cook until tender.
- Add crème fraiche and pesto. Stir to cook the sauce.
- Add lemon juice. Transfer into a serving plate.
- Top with basil leaves and serve.

Tomato and Cheese Salad

Fresh and simple, this low carbohydrate snack or appetizer is a must-try. Only 107 calories per serving.

Ingredients:
(Good for 1 serving)
- 1 large tomato, sliced
- 25 grams of feta cheese
- 1 teaspoon of olive oil

How to make:
- Toss everything in a small bowl and enjoy

Fresh Fruits with Greek Yogurt Dip

Another low calorie Mediterranean-inspired snack or dessert packed with fat-burning nutrients.

Ingredients:
(Good for 1 serving)
- 1 cup of mixed fresh fruits
- ½ cup of low fat Greek yogurt

How to make:
- Arrange the sliced fresh fruits around a bowl.
- Spoon the yogurt dip in the middle of the bowl and serve.

Tuna and Crackers

As you may have noticed, fishes like tuna are important ingredients in the Mediterranean diet. It is a healthy source of both protein and fats that help build lean muscles while promoting weight loss.

Ingredients:
(Good for 1 serving)
- 1 small tin of tuna chunks packed in water, drained
- 4 whole wheat crackers

How to make:
- Simply spoon tuna chunks on crackers and enjoy. Simple yet very flavorful.

Mediterranean Eggs

This is a great power-packed breakfast you can eat all day.

Ingredients:
(Good for 4 servings)
- 4-5 small yellow onions, sliced
- 1 tablespoon of extra virgin olive oil
- 1 tablespoon of butter
- 1 clove garlic, minced
- ⅓ cup of firmly packed julienned sun-dried tomatoes
- 3 ounces of crumbled feta cheese
- 7 large eggs
- salt and fresh ground black pepper

How to make:
- Heat oil and butter in a pan over medium heat. Add onions and sauté over low heat until soft.
- Add tomatoes and garlic. Cook until fragrant. Arrange everything in a single layer and crack the eggs carefully on top of sautéed vegetables.
- Sprinkle the crumbled feta. Season with some pepper and salt.
- Cover and cook for 10-15 minutes until eggs start to set.

- Remove from heat and sprinkle some chopped parsley (optional).

Garlic-Mushroom Kebabs

With the meaty flavor of mushrooms, you won't miss real meat in this recipe.

Ingredients:
(Good for 6 servings)
- 1 pound of cremini mushrooms
- 3 cloves of garlic, crushed
- 2 tablespoons of olive oil
- 1/4 cup of balsamic vinegar
- 1/2 teaspoon of dried basil
- 1/2 teaspoon of dried oregano
- 2 tablespoons of fresh parsley leaves, chopped
- salt and black pepper, to taste

How to make:
- Heat oven to 425 degrees. Lightly coat a baking sheet with cooking spray.

- Whisk olive oil, basil, oregano, garlic and balsamic vinegar. Season to taste with a small amount of pepper and salt. Add the mushrooms and stir. Set aside or 10-15 minutes.
- Insert a skewer into the mushrooms. Bake until softened.
- Garnish with parsley upon serving.

Mediterranean Kale

Here is a recipe to get you to eat more kale. This leafy vegetable is a powerhouse of fat-burning nutrients.

Ingredients:
(Good for 6 servings)
- 12 cups of kale, chopped
- 2 tablespoons of fresh lemon juice
- 1 tablespoon of finely minced garlic
- 1 tablespoon of olive oil
- 1 teaspoon of soy sauce
- Black pepper, ground
- Salt

How to make:
- Steam kale until softened.
- Whisk olive oil, soy sauce, garlic and lemon juice.
- Season with a small amount of pepper and salt.
- Add kale and toss to coat well. Serve.

Insalata Caprese

This simple salad can be your go-to dish on busy days or when you want to whip up something fancy in a jiffy.

Ingredients:
(Good for 6 servings)
- 1 pound of fresh mozzarella cheese, cut into ¼-inch thick sliced
- 4 large tomatoes, ripe, cut into 1/4 –inch thick sections
- 3 tablespoons of extra virgin olive oil
- 1/3 cup of basil leaves, fresh
- Pepper and salt to taste

How to make:
- Arrange in alternate and overlapping manner the cheese slices, basil leaves and tomato slices.
- Drizzle with extra virgin olive oil.
- Sprinkle salt and fresh ground pepper. Serve.

Zucchini and Goat Cheese Frittata

Snack on these low calorie Mediterranean dish that you can whip up in less than 30 minutes.

Ingredients:
(Good for 4 servings)
- 8 eggs
- 2 medium zucchini, sliced   into 1/4-inch rounds
- 2 oz. crumbled goat cheese
- 2 tablespoons of milk
- 1 clove of garlic, crushed
- 1/8 teaspoon of pepper
- 1/4 teaspoon of salt
- 1 tablespoon of olive oil

How to make:
- Heat oven to 350 degrees.
- Whisk milk, eggs, pepper and salt.

- Sauté garlic in oil. Add zucchini. Cook for another 5 minutes.
- Pour egg mixture over the zucchini. Stir for a minute.
- Add cheese and bake in the oven until eggs are set.
- Cool and slice into 4 wedges.

Mediterranean Egg Scramble

Another healthy egg recipe to power up your metabolism.

Ingredients:
(Good for 4 servings)
- 6 eggs
- 1/4 cup of fresh ricotta cheese
- 1 teaspoon of butter
- 1 teaspoon olive oil
- 3 medium-sized new potatoes, thinly sliced
- 8 black olives, chopped
- 1/4 large red bell pepper, small diced
- 1/4 cup fresh parsley, chopped
- Salt and pepper to taste

- 4 slices crusty bread, slightly toasted

How to make:
- Heat oil and butter in a skillet. Add potatoes and sauté until golden.
- Add olives and pepper. Cook for another 4 minutes.
- Whisk eggs, ricotta and parsley. Pour into the pan.
- Cook until eggs are set.
- Sprinkle pepper and salt. Serve with toasted bread.

Savory Fava Beans with Warm Pita Bread

Try this recipe for a new twist on beans.
Ingredients:
(Good for 4 servings)
- 1 15-oz. can fava beans, undrained
- 1 1/2 tablespoons of olive oil
- 1 large tomato, diced
- 1 large onion, sliced
- 1 clove garlic, crushed
- 1 teaspoon of ground cumin
- 1/4 cup of lemon juice
- 1/4 cup of fresh parsley, chopped
- Crushed red pepper flakes, to taste

- Salt and pepper to taste
- 4 whole grain pita bread pockets

How to make;
- Sauté garlic, onions and tomatoes in oil until soft.
- Add fava beans with the liquid and bring to a boil. Lower heat and add lemon juice, parsley and cumin. Season with red pepper, ground pepper and salt.
- Cook for 5 minutes.
- Warm pita and serve with the beans.

Caramelized Figs with Yogurt

This recipe uses honey for a healthier dish.

Ingredients:
(Good for 4 servings)
- 8 ounces fresh figs, halved
- 1 tablespoon honey, plus more for drizzling
- 2 cups plain low-fat Greek yogurt
- 1/4 cup chopped pistachios
- Pinch ground cinnamon

How to make:
- Heat honey and add figs. Cook for 5 minutes.
- Place in a bowl and top with yogurt, cinnamon and pistachios.

Steamed Salmon with Avocado

Get the full benefits of fats in salmon by steaming it. Add avocados and get a better balance between omega-3s and oomega-6s.

Ingredients:
(Good for 4 servings)
- 4 salmon fillets
- 2 lemons, 1 sliced into thin rounds, 1 sliced into wedges
- 1 ripe Hass avocado, thinly sliced
- Fleur de sel

How to make:
- Arrange lemon rounds at the base of a steamer basket.
- Season salmon with fleur de sel and place on top of lemon rounds.
- Stem until fish flakes with a spoon.

- Serve alongside avocado slices and lemon wedges.

Mediterranean Style Smoothie

Make this as an energizing breakfast or snack.

Ingredients:
(Good for 1 serving)
- 1 cup of black seedless grapes
- 1 cup of fresh strawberries
- 1 cup of green seedless grapes
- 1 medium ripe banana
- 1 tablespoon of honey
- ½ cup of plain yogurt

How to make:
- Place all ingredients in a blender and pulse until smooth.
- Pour in a glass and enjoy.

Almond and Date Smoothies

This is another refreshing weight loss smoothie inspired by Mediterranean flavors.

Ingredients:
(Good for 2 servings)
- 4 pitted dates (preferably Medjool)
- 3 tablespoons almond butter
- 1 cup low-fat plain yogurt
- 1 cup apple cider or apple juice

How to make:
- Place all ingredients in a blender and pulse until smooth.
- Pour in glass and serve.

Conclusion

Thank you again for reading this book!

I hope this book was able to help you to lose weight with the Mediterranean diet.

The next step is to start making the recipes given in this book and eat your way into a leaner and fitter you.

If you have enjoyed this book, please be sure to leave a review and a comment to let us know how we are doing so we can continue to bring you quality books.

Thank you and good luck!

Book 2: Mediterranean Diet

The Mediterranean Diet Cookbook with Delicious Recipes for Weight Loss

Introduction

First of all, I would like to thank you for opening this book and congratulations on your decision to become healthier.

In this book, you will learn all about the Mediterranean Diet and how it can help you achieve your weight goals without limiting your diet. In the following chapter, you will learn about the basics of Mediterranean Diet and how you can change some foods in your diet to turn it into a healthy Mediterranean meal. You'll be surprised how easy following this diet plan is.

Of course, a diet manual will not be complete without mouthwatering recipes that are both healthy and easy to prepare. The great thing about Mediterranean diet is that you don't have to have extensive knowledge in cooking to prepare the right meals. Heck, you don't even have to do much cooking.

I hope this book will help you reach your health goals. Thanks again for reading and I hope you enjoy the recipes as much as I do.

Chapter 1 – The Mediterranean Diet at a Glance

The Mediterranean Diet is called as such because it consists of the traditional healthy lifestyle of people from countries surrounding the beautiful Mediterranean Sea such as Spain, Greece, France, and Italy. The Mediterranean cuisine slightly varies by region but the staple ingredients are mostly the same. Foods from these regions are mostly based on fish, olive oil, cereal grains, beans, nuts, fruits, and vegetables.

The Mediterranean diet has always been associated with healthy living and has been proven to lower the risk of stroke and heart disease by 30%. To make your diet more Mediterranean, you can add more starchy foods like pasta and bread, eat more vegetables and fruits, add fish and lessen the meat intake. It's also advisable to choose products derived from vegetables and plants such as olive oil.

To achieve a well-balanced diet while working on your set weight goals, you should base your meals on starchy carbohydrates like potatoes, rice, pasta, or bread. Pick the whole grain varieties whenever you can for more fiber. For fruits and vegetables, it is highly recommended to take at least 5 portions per day to boost your metabolism.

When it comes to protein, choose lean meat, fish, beans, or eggs. Add some milk and dairy like yogurt and cheese for calcium and additional protein. If possible, avoid eating sugary foods or foods with high fat content.

Switching to a Mediterranean diet is easier than you think. It would be a great start if you would strive to get the recommended diet every day. To help you begin, I've included great plus their recipes nutritional information so you can get a gist of how a Mediterranean meal is like.

Chapter 2 – Flavorful Mediterranean Salads

1. Tuscan Tuna Salad

**This recipe makes 4 servings. Each serving has 199 Calories, 9g Fats, 20g Carbohydrates, 16g Protein, and 17mg Cholesterol.

Ingredients:

- 10 cherry tomatoes, quartered
- 2 (6 oz.) cans of light chunk tuna, drain
- 2 tablespoons of extra-virgin olive oil
- 4 scallions, trim and slice
- ¼ teaspoon of salt
- 2 tablespoons of lemon juice
- freshly ground pepper
- 1 (15 oz.) can of small white beans

Directions:

1. Add all the ingredients in a bowl and mix gently. Refrigerate until serving time.

2. Tuna Antipasto Salad

**This recipe makes 4 servings. Each serving has 306 Calories, 16g Fats, 28g Carbohydrates, 15g Protein, and 15mg Cholesterol.

Ingredients:

- 2 (6 oz.) cans of light chunk tuna in water, drain and flake
- 1 (19 oz.) can of beans
- ½ cup of fine chopped red onion
- 1 large red bell pepper, diced finely
- 4 teaspoons of capers, rinsed
- ½ cup of chopped fresh parsley
- ½ cup of lemon juice
- ½ teaspoons of fine chopped fresh rosemary
- freshly ground pepper
- 4 tablespoons of extra-virgin olive oil
- 8 cups of mixed salad greens
- ¼ teaspoon of salt

Directions:

1. Mix together 2 tablespoons of olive oil, ¼ cup of lemon juice, rosemary, capers, parsley, onion, bell pepper,

tuna, and beans. Season the mixture with pepper.

2. Mix the remaining lemon juice, olive oil and salt. Add in the greens and toss until well-coated. Divide the greens into 4 serving plates and top each with the salad.

3. *Garden Pasta Salad*

**This recipe makes 6 servings. Each serving has 217 Calories, 9g Fats, 30g Carbohydrates, 6g Protein, and 4mg Cholesterol.

Ingredients:

- ⅓ cup of reduced-fat mayonnaise
- 2 cups of whole-wheat rotini
- 2 tablespoons of extra-virgin olive oil
- ⅓ cup of low-fat plain yogurt
- 1 clove of garlic, mince
- 1 tablespoon of red wine vinegar
- 1 cup of cherry tomatoes, cut in half
- ⅛ teaspoon of salt
- 1 cup of diced red bell pepper
- freshly ground pepper
- ½ cup of chopped and pitted Kalamata olives
- 1 cup of grated carrots
- ⅓ cup of slivered fresh basil
- ½ cup of chopped scallions

Directions:

1. Prepare the pasta based on the package directions.

2. Whisk together the pepper, salt, garlic, red wine vinegar, olive oil, yogurt, and mayonnaise until smooth. Add in the pasta and toss until well-coated. Add the basil, olives, scallions, carrots, bell pepper, and tomatoes. Mix well.

4. *Greek Sardine Salad*

**This recipe makes 4 servings. Each serving has 347 Calories, 18g Fats, 29g Carbohydrates, 17g Protein, and 67mg Cholesterol.

Ingredients:

- 2 tablespoons of extra-virgin olive oil
- 3 tablespoons of lemon juice
- 2 teaspoons of dried oregano
- 1 clove of garlic, mince
- 3 medium tomatoes, cut into chunks
- ½ teaspoon of freshly ground pepper
- 1 (15 oz.) can of chickpeas, rinsed
- 1 large English cucumber, cut into chunks
- ¼ cup of thin sliced red onion
- ⅓ cup of crumbled feta cheese
- 2 (4 oz.) cans of sardines in olive oil, drained
- 2 tablespoons of sliced Kalamata olives

Directions:

1. Whisk together the pepper, oregano, garlic, oil, and lemon juice in a bowl.

2. Add in the olives, onion, cheese, chickpeas, cucumber, and tomatoes.

3. Toss gently until well-combined. Top with sardines and serve.

5. *Black Eyed Peas & Cucumber Salad*

**This recipe makes 6 servings. Each serving has 161 Calories, 10g Fats, 12g Carbohydrates, 5g Protein, and 11mg Cholesterol.

Ingredients:

- 2 tablespoons of lemon juice
- 3 tablespoons of extra-virgin olive oil
- freshly ground pepper
- 2 teaspoons of chopped fresh oregano
- 1 (14 oz.) can of black-eyed peas, rinse
- 4 cups of diced cucumbers
- ½ cup of crumble feta cheese
- ⅔ cup of diced red bell pepper
- 2 tablespoons of chopped black olives
- ¼ cup of slivered red onion

Directions:

1. Whisk together the pepper, oregano, lemon juice, and oil.

2. Add in the olives, onion, cheese, bell pepper, black-eyed peas, and cucumber.

3. Toss until the ingredients are well-coated.

6. Bean & Pita Salad

**This recipe makes 4 servings. Each serving has 427 Calories, 21g Fats, 46g Carbohydrates, 17g Protein, and 33mg Cholesterol.

Ingredients:

- 2 cloves of garlic, peeled
- 2 (6 in) whole wheat pita, cut to bite-size pieces
- 2 tablespoons of fresh lemon juice
- ⅛ teaspoon of salt
- 3 tablespoons of extra-virgin olive oil
- 2 tablespoons of ground toasted cumin seeds
- 2 cups of cooked pinto beans, drain well and warm slightly
- freshly ground pepper
- ½ cucumber, peel and dice
- 1 cup of diced plum tomatoes
- 1 cup of crumbled feta cheese
- 1 cup of sliced romaine lettuce
- 3 tablespoons of chopped fresh mint
- 3 tablespoons of chopped fresh parsley

Directions:

1. Turn on oven and set to 400F.

2. Spread the pieces of pita bread on a baking sheet. Bake in the oven for 7 minutes. Let cool.

3. Mash the salt and garlic to form a paste. Transfer the paste into a bowl and whisk in the cumin and lemon juice. Add in the oil in a slow and steady stream while whisking. Season with pepper.

4. Mix together the cucumber, tomatoes, and beans in a salad bowl. Add in the dressing, mint, parsley, cheese, lettuce, and pita. Toss until well-combined and season accordingly. Serve.

7. Ripe Olive & Artichoke Tuna Salad

**This recipe makes 5 servings. Each serving has 103 Calories, 5g Fats, 8g Carbohydrates, 8g Protein, and 16mg Cholesterol.

Ingredients:

- 1 cup of chopped artichoke hearts
- 1 (12 oz.) can of light chunk tuna, drain and flake
- ⅓ cup of reduced-fat mayonnaise
- ½ cup of chopped olives
- 1 ½ teaspoons of chopped fresh oregano
- 2 teaspoons of lemon juice

Directions:

1. Mix together all the ingredients in a bowl and serve.

8. Chicken Greek Salad

**This recipe makes 2 servings. Each serving has 343 Calories, 18g Fats, 11g Carbohydrates, 31g Protein, and 89mg Cholesterol.

Ingredients:

- 1 tablespoon of extra-virgin olive oil
- 2 ½ tablespoons of red wine vinegar
- ½ teaspoon of garlic powder
- 1 ½ teaspoons of chopped fresh dill
- ⅛ teaspoon of freshly ground pepper
- ⅛ teaspoon of salt
- 1 ¼ cups of chopped cooked chicken
- 3 cups of chopped romaine lettuce
- ½ medium cucumber, peel, deseed, and chop
- 1 medium tomato, chop
- ¼ cup of sliced ripe black olives
- ¼ cup of fine chopped red onion
- ¼ cup of crumbled feta cheese

Directions:

1. Whisk together the pepper, salt, garlic powder, dill, olive oil, and red wine vinegar in a salad bowl.

2. Add in the cheese, olives, onion, cucumber, tomato, chicken, and lettuce. Toss until well-coated.

9. Orzo Salad

**This recipe makes 2 servings. Each recipe has 436 Calories, 8g Fats, 73g Carbohydrates, 19g Protein, and 5mg Cholesterol.

Ingredients:

- 1 ½ teaspoons of extra-virgin olive oil
- ½ cup of orzo
- ⅛ teaspoon of salt
- 1 clove of garlic, crush and peel
- ⅛ teaspoon of freshly ground pepper
- 1 ½ tablespoons of lemon juice
- 1 (7 oz.) can of chickpeas, rinse
- 1 (14 oz.) can of artichoke hearts, drain and chop
- 2 tablespoons of chopped fresh dill
- ⅓ cup of crumbled feta cheese
- 1 large tomato, chopped
- 1 ½ tablespoons of chopped fresh mint
- 2 cups of baby spinach leaves

Directions:

1. Prepare the orzo according to package directions.

2. Mash the garlic together until a paste forms. Whisk in the pepper and lemon juice. Add in the mint, dill, cheese, chickpeas, artichokes and orzo. Gently toss until combined. Mix in the tomatoes.

3. Arrange the spinach in a salad bowl and set the salad on top.

10. Lentil Lemony Salad

**This recipe makes 6 servings. Each serving has 354 Calories, 18g Fats, 24g Carbohydrates, 24g Protein, and 31mg Cholesterol.

Ingredients:

- ⅓ cup of chopped fresh dill
- ⅓ cup of lemon juice
- ¼ teaspoon of salt
- 2 teaspoons of Dijon mustard
- ⅓ cup of extra-virgin olive oil
- freshly ground pepper
- 1 cup of diced seedless cucumber
- 1 medium red bell pepper, deseed then dice
- 2 (15 oz.) cans of lentils, rinse
- ½ cup of fine chopped red onion
- 2 (7 oz.) cans of salmon, drain then flake

Directions:

1. Whisk together the pepper, salt, mustard, dill, and lemon juice. Pour in the olive oil while whisking.

2. Add in the salmon, lentils, onion, cucumber, and bell pepper. Toss together until well-coated.

11. *White Bean Tuna Salad*

**This recipe makes 4 servings. Each serving has 223 Calories, 7g Fats, 23g Carbohydrates, 17g Protein, and 15mg Cholesterol.

Ingredients:

- 2 tablespoons of extra-virgin olive oil
- 3 tablespoons of lemon juice
- ⅛ teaspoon of salt
- 1 clove of garlic, mince
- 1 (19 oz.) can of cannellini, rinse
- freshly ground pepper
- 3 tablespoons of chopped fresh parsley
- ¼ cup of chopped red onion
- 1 (6 oz.) can of light chunk tuna in water, drain and flake

Directions:

1. Whisk together the pepper, salt, garlic, oil, and lemon juice.

2. Add in the basil, parsley, onion, tuna, and beans. Toss together until well-coated.

12. *Salmon Panzanella*

**This recipe makes 4 servings. Each serving has 320 Calories, 18g Fats, 53mg Cholesterol, 26g Protein, and 53mg Cholesterol.

Ingredients:

- 3 tablespoons of red wine vinegar
- 8 Kalamata olives, remove pits then chop
- ¼ teaspoon of freshly ground pepper
- 1 tablespoon of capers, rinse then chop
- 2 slices of day-old wheat bread, cut into cubes
- 3 tablespoons of extra-virgin olive oil
- 1 medium cucumber, peel then deseed and cut into cubes
- 2 large tomatoes, cut into cubes
- ¼ cup of thin sliced fresh basil
- ¼ cup of thin sliced red onion
- ½ teaspoon of kosher salt
- 1 lb. of center-cut salmon, skin and divide to 4 equal portions

Directions:

1. Set the grill to high.

2. Whisk together half of the pepper, capers, red wine vinegar, and olives. Pour in the oil while whisking. Add in the basil, onion, cucumber, tomatoes, and bread. Mix well.

3. Grease the grill rack and season the salmon with the remaining pepper and salt. Grill each side for 5 minutes.

4. Assemble the salad and top with salmon.

13. Grilled Tofu Salad

**This recipe makes 4 servings. Each serving has 209 Calories, 16g Fats, 10g Carbohydrates, 9g Protein, and 0mg Cholesterol.

Ingredients:

- 1 tablespoon of extra-virgin olive oil
- ¼ cup of lemon juice
- 2 teaspoons of dried oregano
- 3 cloves of garlic, mince
- 14 oz. of extra-firm tofu
- ½ teaspoon of salt
- freshly ground pepper

Directions:

1. Heat the grill.

2. Whisk together the pepper, salt, oregano, garlic, oil, and lemon juice in a mixing bowl. Reserve 2 tablespoons of the mixture.

3. Drain then rinse the tofu and pat dry. Cut the tofu crosswise to make 8 ½-inch thick pieces. Place in a glass dish. Add the reserved mixture

and turn to coat well. Cover and refrigerate for 8 hours.

4. Grease the grill rack and drain the tofu. Grill each side over medium-high heat for 4 minutes.

5. Place on top of your favorite salad.

14. Shrimp on White Bean Salad

**This recipe makes 6 servings. Each serving has 212 Calories, 8g Fats, 22g Carbohydrates, 17g Protein, and 95mg Cholesterol.

Ingredients:

- ⅓ cup of lemon juice
- 1 teaspoon of fine grated lemon zest
- 2 tablespoons of packed fresh oregano, mince
- 3 tablespoons of extra-virgin olive oil
- 2 tablespoons of minced fresh chives
- 2 tablespoons of packed fresh sage, mince
- ½ teaspoon of salt
- 1 teaspoon of freshly ground pepper
- 12 cherry tomatoes, quartered
- 2 (15 oz.) cans of cannellini beans, rinse
- 24 raw shrimp, peel and devein
- 1 cup of finely diced celery

Directions:

1. Mix together the salt, pepper, chives, sage, oregano, oil, lemon juice, and lemon zest in a bowl.

Reserve 2 tablespoons of this mixture and place in a small bowl. Add in the celery, tomatoes, and beans. Mix well.

2. Set a grill pan over medium-high heat.

3. Thread the shrimps on 6 skewers. Grease the grill pan then cook the shrimp about 4 minutes each side. Serve on top of the salad and drizzle the reserved dressing on top.

15. *Antipasto Salad*

**This recipe makes 2 servings. Each serving has 343 Calories, 16g Fats, 33g Carbohydrates, 19g Protein, and 20mg Cholesterol.

Ingredients:

- 1 (6 oz.) can of light chunk tuna in water, drain then flake
- ½ (19 oz.) can of beans, rinse
- ¼ cup of fine chopped red onion
- ½ large red bell pepper, diced finely
- 2 teaspoons of capers, rinse
- ¼ cup of chopped fresh parsley
- 4 tablespoons of lemon juice
- ¾ teaspoon of fine chopped fresh rosemary
- freshly ground pepper
- 2 tablespoons of extra-virgin olive oil
- 4 cups of mixed salad greens
- ⅛ teaspoon of salt

Directions:

1. Mix together 1 tablespoon of olive oil, 2 tablespoons of lemon juice, rosemary, capers, parsley, onion,

bell pepper, tuna, and beans in a salad bowl.

2. Season the mixture with pepper.

3. Mix together the remaining lemon juice and olive oil in a bowl. Add salt and the salad greens. Toss until well-coated. Top with the tuna mixture. Serve.

16. Tuna & Pepper Pasta Salad

**This recipe makes 4 servings. Each serving has 258 Calories, 5g Fats, 39g Carbohydrates, 16g Protein, and 15mg Cholesterol.

Ingredients:

- 1 (7 oz.) jar of roasted red peppers, rinse and slice
- 1 (6 oz.) can of light chunk tuna in water, drain
- 2 tablespoons of capers, rinse and chop coarsely
- ½ cup of fine chopped red onion
- 2 tablespoons of chopped fresh basil
- 2 tablespoons of nonfat plain yogurt
- 1 ½ teaspoons of lemon juice
- 1 tablespoon of extra-virgin olive oil
- ⅛ teaspoon of salt
- 1 small clove of garlic, crush and peel
- 1 ¾ cups of whole wheat penne
- freshly ground pepper

Directions:

1. Prepare the pasta according to package directions.

2. Mix together the capers, red onion, tuna, and ⅓ cup of roasted red peppers in a bowl.

3. Mix the basil, yogurt, lemon juice, olive oil, salt, garlic, pepper, and the remaining roasted red peppers using a blender. Puree until the mixture becomes smooth.

4. Combine the pasta and tuna mixture and pour the roasted red pepper sauce. Toss until well-combined.

17. Meat & Veggie Warm Salad

**This recipe makes 4 servings. Each serving has 271 Calories, 15g Fats, 26g Carbohydrates, 10g Protein, and 16mg Cholesterol.

Ingredients:

- 1 lb. of new potatoes, scrub then cut to ¾-inch chunks
- 1 lb. of mustard greens, trim and wash then chop coarsely
- 2 teaspoons of fennel seeds
- ½ lb. of hot Italian sausage, remove casing
- 2 tablespoons red wine vinegar
- 2 tablespoons of extra-virgin olive oil
- ¼ teaspoon of salt
- 1 small clove of garlic, mince
- freshly ground pepper

Directions:

1. Add 2 cups of salted water in a wide pan and bring to boil. Add in the mustard greens and cover with a lid. Cook for 5 minutes over medium heat. Stir in the potatoes and add another ½ cup of water. Replace the

lid and cook for another 10 minutes. Drain and place the vegetables in a bowl.

2. Cook the sausage and fennel seeds over medium heat for 12 minutes. Drain then cut the sausage into bite-size pieces. Add into the bowl with vegetables.

3. Whisk together the pepper, salt, garlic, red wine vinegar, and olive oil. Pour into the bowl and toss until well-combined. Serve.

18. Chickpea Salad

**This recipe makes 6 servings. Each serving has 81 Calories, 2g Fats, 12g Carbohydrates, 4g Protein, 3mg Cholesterol.

Ingredients:

For the dressing

- ¾ cup of nonfat cottage cheese
- 1 small shallot, peel
- 2 tablespoons of buttermilk powder
- ¼ cup of reduced fat mayonnaise
- ¼ cup of nonfat milk
- 2 tablespoons of white wine vinegar
- ¼ teaspoon of salt
- 1 tablespoon of chopped dill
- ¼ teaspoon of freshly ground pepper

For the salad

- 3 cups of diced cucumber
- 1 (7 oz.) can of chickpeas, rinse
- ¼ cup of crumbled feta cheese
- 2 cups of halved grape tomatoes
- ½ cup of ranch dressing
- ¼ cup of diced red onion
- freshly ground pepper

Directions:

1. Mix all the ingredients for the dressing in a food processor. Process until smooth and well-combined.

2. Mix the onion, cheese, tomatoes, cucumber, and chickpeas in a salad bowl. Add in the dressing and season with pepper. Toss until well-coated.

19. Tomato & Bread Salad

**This recipe makes 6 servings. Each serving has 156 Calories, 9g Fats, 18g Carbohydrates, 3g Protein, and 0mg Cholesterol.

Ingredients:

- 3 tablespoons of lemon juice
- 3 tablespoons of extra-virgin olive oil
- ¼ teaspoon of salt
- 1 small clove of garlic, mince
- 4 cups of diced tomatoes
- freshly ground pepper
- ¼ cup of thin slivered red onion
- 2 cups of cubed whole wheat bread, remove crusts
- 2 tablespoons of capers, rinse
- 3 tablespoons of chopped fresh basil
- 4 (4 ½ oz.) cans of sardines

Directions:

1. Whisk together the pepper, salt, garlic, lemon juice, and olive oil in a bowl.

2. Add in the capers, basil, onion, bread, and tomatoes. Toss until well

combined. Sit for 5 minutes before serving.

20. Mixed Green & Cheese Salad

**This recipe makes 8 servings. Each serving has 133 Calories, 10g Fats, 1g Carbohydrates, 3g Protein, and 13mg Cholesterol.

Ingredients:

For the dressing

- 2 tablespoons of red wine vinegar
- ¼ cup of extra-virgin olive oil
- ¼ teaspoon of salt

For the salad

- 8 cups of mesclun salad greens
- freshly ground pepper
- 2 cups of halved seedless grapes
- 1 head of radicchio, sliced thinly
- ¾ cup of crumbled feta cheese

Directions:

1. Whisk together all the ingredients for the dressing.

2. Toss together the salad greens and radicchio in a salad bowl. Drizzle the dressing and toss until well-coated.

Scatter the cheese and grapes over the salad and serve.

21. Shrimp Panzanella

**This recipe makes 6 servings. Each serving has 264 Calories, 13g Fats, 21g Carbohydrates, 16g Protein, and 95mg Cholesterol.

Ingredients:

- 1 clove of garlic, peel and cut in half
- 4 tablespoons of extra-virgin olive oil
- 1 lb. of coarsely chopped cooked shrimp
- 4 cups of crusty multigrain bread cubes
- 2 large green bell peppers, chopped
- 4 large ripe tomatoes, coarsely chopped
- ¼ cup of chopped fresh chives
- ¾ cup of chopped fresh parsley
- 3 tablespoons of red wine vinegar
- ¼ cup of sliced pitted Kalamata olives
- ¼ cup of olive brine
- freshly ground pepper
- 1 ½ teaspoons of chopped fresh thyme
- 4 cups of mixed salad greens

Directions:

1. Turn on oven and set to 350F.

2. Grease a rimmed baking sheet using 2 tablespoons of olive oil. Mash the garlic into the oil then discard the garlic. Stir in the bread into the oil until lightly coated. Bake in the oven for 15 minutes, stirring every 5 minutes. Cool completely.

3. Mix the remaining olive oil, thyme, vinegar, brine, olives, chives, parsley, bell peppers, tomatoes, and shrimp. Season the mixture with pepper and let stand for 10 minutes to marinate.

4. Toss in the croutons into the shrimp mix and serve over the mixed greens.

22. Pesto Chicken Salad

**This recipe makes 4 servings. Each serving has 324 Calories, 20g Fats, 9g Carbohydrates, 27g Protein, and 71mg Cholesterol.

Ingredients:

- ¼ cup of pesto
- 1 lb. of boneless and skinless chicken breast, trim
- 3 tablespoons of fine chopped red onion
- ¼ cup of low fat mayonnaise
- 2 tablespoons of red wine vinegar
- 2 tablespoons of extra-virgin olive oil
- ¼ teaspoon of ground pepper
- ¼ teaspoon of salt
- 1 pint of grape tomatoes, cut in half
- 1 (5 oz.) pack of mixed salad greens

Directions:

1. Place the chicken in a saucepan and cover with water. Bring to boil. Cover with a lid and adjust the heat to low. Simmer for 15 minutes. Transfer the chicken into a chopping board and shred to bite size pieces.

2. Mix together the onion, mayonnaise and pest. Add in the shredded chicken and toss until well-coated. Whisk together the olive oil, red wine vinegar, pepper, and salt. Add in the tomatoes and salad greens and toss until well-coated. Top with the chicken salad and serve.

23. *Warm Arugula Salad*

**This recipe makes 4 servings. Each serving has 197 Calories, 12g Fats, 16g Carbohydrates, 6g Protein, and 4mg Cholesterol.

Ingredients:

- 2 slices of crusty whole wheat bread, cut into cubes
- 3 tablespoons of extra-virgin olive oil
- 8 cups of arugula
- 1 cup of cherry tomatoes, cut in half
- ⅛ teaspoon of salt
- 1 tablespoon of minced garlic
- 2 tablespoons of balsamic vinegar
- ⅛ teaspoon of freshly ground pepper
- ¼ cup of parmesan cheese, shave

Directions:

1. Heat 2 tablespoons of the olive oil in a large pan set over medium-high heat. Stir in the bread cubes and cook for 6 minutes while stirring occasionally. Add in the arugula and tomatoes and cook for a minute.

Push the mixture to one side of the pan.

2. Add the remaining olive oil into the pan and cook the garlic for 15 seconds. Stir in the bread mixture and remove the pan from heat. Drizzle with vinegar and season with pepper and salt. Toss until well-combined and serve immediately topped with the cheese.

24. Tarragon Spring Salad

**This recipe makes 2 servings. Each serving has 358 Calories, 26g Fats, 9g Carbohydrates, 23g Protein, and 262mg Cholesterol.

Ingredients:

- 2 tablespoons of extra-virgin olive oil
- 2 tablespoons of red wine vinegar
- ¼ teaspoon of dried tarragon
- 1 teaspoon of whole grain mustard
- 1 pinch of freshly ground pepper
- 1 pinch of salt
- ½ bunch of asparagus, remove tough ends
- 1 clove of garlic, crush
- 1 (5 oz.) bag of mixed salad greens
- 2 large hard-boiled eggs
- 1 (4 oz.) can of sardines, drained
- 10 cherry tomatoes
- 6 olives

Directions:

1. Whisk together the salt, pepper, tarragon, mustard, olive oil, and red wine vinegar. Add in the garlic and set aside.

2. Fill a medium pan with 1 inch of water and let it boil. Add in the asparagus and cook for 3 minutes. Drain and place under running water to cool.

3. Peel and slice the eggs. Assemble the salad greens and top with the olives, sardines, tomatoes, asparagus, and eggs. Remove the garlic from the dressing and stir to combine. Drizzle over the salad before serving.

25. *Orange Fennel Salad*

**This recipe makes 4 servings. Each serving has 181 Calories, 12g Fats, 17g Carbohydrates, 4g Protein, and 0mg Cholesterol.

Ingredients:

- 1 small bulb of fennel, quarter and core then thinly slice crosswise
- 2 navel oranges, peel and quarter then thinly slice
- ¼ cup of coarsely chopped fresh cilantro
- 1 cup of very thin sliced radishes
- 1 tablespoon and 1 teaspoon of lime juice
- 2 tablespoons of extra-virgin olive oil
- freshly ground pepper
- ¼ teaspoon of salt
- 6 tablespoons of shelled pistachio nuts, toast and chop

Directions:

1. Mix the salt, pepper, olive oil, lime juice, cilantro, radishes, fennel, and orange slices in a bowl.

2. Sprinkle nuts on top of the salad and serve.

Chapter 3 – Quick and Easy Mediterranean Entrees

1. Creamy Garlic Shrimp Pasta

**This recipe makes 4 servings. Each serving has 361 Calories, 6g Fats, 53g Carbohydrates, 28g Protein, and 108mg Cholesterol.

Ingredients:

- 12 oz. of raw shrimp, peel and devein
- 6 oz. of whole wheat spaghetti
- 1 large red bell pepper, slice thinly
- 1 bunch of asparagus, trim and slice thinly
- 3 cloves of garlic, chop
- 1 cup of fresh peas
- 1 ½ cups of nonfat plain yogurt
- 1 ¼ teaspoons of kosher salt
- 3 tablespoons of lemon juice
- ¼ cup of chopped flat-leaf parsley
- ½ teaspoon of freshly ground pepper
- 1 tablespoon of extra-virgin olive oil
- ¼ cup of toasted pine nuts

Directions:

1. Cook the spaghetti according to package directions.

2. Fill a large pot with water and bring to boil. Add in the peas, bell pepper, asparagus, and shrimp and cook for 4 minutes. Drain well.

3. Mash the salt and garlic into paste. Whisk in the pepper, olive oil, lemon juice, parsley, and yogurt. Add in the pasta and toss to combine. Top with the pine nuts and serve.

2. Lasagna

**This recipe makes 4 servings. Each serving has 338 Calories, 9g Fats, 53g Carbohydrates, 18g Protein, and 14mg Cholesterol.

Ingredients:

- 1 tablespoon of extra-virgin olive oil
- 8 oz. of whole-wheat rotini
- 3 cloves of garlic, slice
- 1 onion, chop
- ½ teaspoon of salt
- 8 oz. of sliced white mushrooms
- 1 (14 oz.) can of diced tomatoes with Italian herbs
- ¼ teaspoon of freshly ground pepper
- ½ teaspoon of crushed red pepper
- 8 cups of baby spinach
- ¾ cup of part-skim ricotta cheese

Directions:

1. Prepare the pasta according to package directions.

2. Set a large skillet over medium heat. Heat the olive oil. Add in the garlic and onion and cook for 3 minutes.

Add in the pepper, salt, and mushrooms and cook for 6 minutes while stirring continuously.

3. Add in the crushed red pepper, spinach and tomatoes. Set the heat to medium-high and cook for 4 minutes.

4. Toss all the ingredients and divide among serving bowls. Top each with 3 tablespoons of ricotta before serving.

3. Gnocchi in Brown Butter

** This recipe makes 4 servings. Each serving has 426 Calories, 11g Fats, 66g Carbohydrates, 17g Protein, and 25mg Cholesterol.

Ingredients:

- 2 tablespoons of butter
- 1lb of fresh gnocchi
- 1 lb. of zucchini, slice lengthwise very thinly
- 2 medium shallots, chop
- ½ teaspoon of salt
- 1 pint of cherry tomatoes, halved
- freshly ground pepper
- ¼ teaspoon grated nutmeg
- ½ cup of chopped fresh parsley
- ½ cup of grated parmesan cheese

Directions:

1. Cook the gnocchi according to package directions. Drain and set aside.

2. Set a large pan over medium-high heat. Melt the butter. Add the zucchini and shallots and cook for 3 minutes. Stir in the pepper, nutmeg,

salt, and tomatoes and cook for another 2 minutes. Stir in the parsley and parmesan. Then, add the gnocchi. Mix well and serve.

4. *Tortellini Primavera*

**This recipe makes 5 servings. Each serving has 426 Calories, 15g Fats, 55g Carbohydrates, 15g Protein, and 68mg Cholesterol.

Ingredients:

- 2 tablespoons of all-purpose flour
- 1 (14 oz.) can of vegetable broth
- 3 cloves of garlic, slice
- 1 tablespoon of extra-virgin olive oil
- 1 tablespoon of chopped fresh tarragon
- 1 cup of shredded fontina cheese
- 4 cups of chopped vegetables
- ⅛ teaspoon of salt
- 1 (16 oz.) pack of frozen cheese tortellini

Directions:

1. Fill a large pot with water then bring to boil.

2. Whisk together the flour and broth in a bowl. Set a large pan over medium heat and add in the olive oil. Once hot, add in the garlic and cook for 2 minutes. Add in the broth

mixture and bring to boil while stirring continuously. Cook for 3 minutes then remove the pan from the heat. Stir in the salt, tarragon, and cheese.

3. Add in the tortellini and vegetables into the pot and simmer for 5 minutes. Drain then add to the pan with the sauce. Mix well.

5. Paprika Bean & Shrimp Sauté

**This recipe makes 6 servings. Each serving has 237 Calories, 8g Fats, 26g Carbohydrates, 23g Protein, and 122mg Cholesterol.

Ingredients:

- 3 tablespoons of extra-virgin olive oil
- 4 cups of green beans, trim
- 2 teaspoons of paprika
- ¼ cup of minced garlic
- 2 (16 oz.) cans of large butter beans, rinse
- 1 lb. of raw shrimp, peel and devein
- ½ teaspoon of salt
- ¼ cup of sherry vinegar
- freshly ground pepper
- ½ cup of chopped fresh parsley.

Directions:

1. Fill a large saucepan with an inch of water and bring to boil. Place the green beans in a steamer basket and place over the saucepan. Cover with a lid and steam for 6 minutes.

2. Set a skillet over medium-high heat and add in the olive oil. Once hot, add the paprika and garlic and cook for 20 seconds. Add in the shrimp and cook each side for 2 minutes. Stir in the salt, vinegar, and beans. Cook for 2 minutes. Stir in half of the parsley.

3. Place the green beans on a salad bowl and top with the shrimp mix. Top with the remaining parsley and season with pepper.

6. Baked Parmesan Potatoes

**This recipe makes 4 servings. Each serving has 86 Calories, 6g Fats, 6g Carbohydrates, 3g Protein, and 4mg Cholesterol.

Ingredients:

- ¼ cup of freshly grated parmesan cheese
- 4 tomatoes, halved
- ¼ teaspoon of salt
- 1 teaspoon of chopped fresh oregano
- freshly ground pepper
- 4 teaspoons of extra-virgin olive oil

Directions:

1. Turn on oven and set to 450F.

2. Place the tomatoes with the cut-side facing up on a baking sheet. Top each tomatoes with the cheese, oregano and season with pepper and salt. Drizzle oil and bake for 15 minutes.

7. Creamy Mushroom & Fettuccine

**This recipe makes 6 servings. Each serving has 384 Calories, 10g Fats, 56g Carbohydrates, 18g Protein, and 21mg Cholesterol.

Ingredients:

- 1 tablespoon of extra-virgin olive oil
- 12 oz. of whole wheat fettuccine
- 4 cups of thin sliced Brussels sprout
- 4 cups of sliced mixed mushrooms
- ½ cup of dry sherry
- 1 tablespoon of minced garlic
- 2 tablespoons of all-purpose flour
- 2 cups of low-fat milk
- ½ teaspoon of freshly ground pepper
- ½ teaspoon of salt
- 1 cup of fine shredded Asiago cheese

Directions:

1. Prepare the pasta according to package directions. Set aside until needed.

---

2. Add oil in a large pan set over medium heat. Add in the Brussels sprout and mushrooms and cook for 10 minutes. Add in the garlic and cook for another minute. Add in the dry sherry and bring to boil. Cook for 10 seconds while scraping up any browned bits.

3. Whisk together the flour and milk in a bowl. Pour the mixture into the pan and add pepper and salt. Cook for 2 minutes. Stir in the Asiago and cook until melted. Add the sauce into the pasta and toss gently. Serve with additional cheese.

8. Tomato & Turkey Panini

**This recipe makes 4 servings. Each serving has 314 Calories, 8g Fats, 37g Carbohydrates, 22g Protein, and 30mg Cholesterol.

Ingredients:

- 2 tablespoons of nonfat plain yogurt
- 3 tablespoons of reduced fat mayonnaise
- 2 tablespoons of chopped fresh basil
- 2 tablespoons of shredded parmesan cheese
- freshly ground pepper
- 1 teaspoon of lemon juice
- 8 slices of tomato
- 8 oz. of thin sliced deli turkey
- 2 teaspoons of canola oil
- 8 slices of whole wheat bread

Directions:

1. Mix the pepper, lemon juice, basil, parmesan, yogurt, and mayonnaise. Spread 2 teaspoons over each bread slice. Divide the tomato and turkey into 4 and place over 4 bread slices. Place the remaining bread slices on top.

2. Add 1 teaspoon of the canola oil in a skillet set over medium heat. Place 2 Panini and flatten using a smaller pan weighed down with cans. Cook each side for 2 minutes. Repeat the same steps with the remaining Paninis.

9. Lemon Dill Chicken

**This recipe makes 4 servings. Each serving has 170 Calories, 6g Fats, 3g Carbohydrates, 24g Protein, and 63mg Cholesterol.

Ingredients:

- Salt
- Freshly ground pepper
- 4 boneless and skinless chicken breasts
- ¼ cup of finely chopped onion
- 3 teaspoons of extra-virgin olive oil
- 1 cup of reduced sodium chicken broth
- 3 cloves of garlic, minced
- 2 tablespoons of chopped fresh dill
- 2 teaspoons of flour
- 1 tablespoon of lemon juice

Directions:

1. Season both sides of the chicken breasts with pepper and salt. Add 1 ½ teaspoons of the olive oil in a heavy skillet and place over medium-high heat. Cook each side of the chicken for 3 minutes. Place

the chicken on a plate and cover with foil.

2. Reduce the heat to medium and add in the remaining olive oil into the heavy skillet. Add in the garlic and onion and cook for 1 minute. Whisk together the lemon juice, 1 tablespoons of dill, flour, and broth and pour it into the skillet. Whisk and cook for 3 minutes.

3. Return the chicken into the skillet and simmer for 4 minutes. Transfer the chicken on a serving platter. Season the sauce with additional pepper and salt then pour over the chicken. Top with the remaining fresh dill.

10. Crusted Salmon

**This recipe makes 4 servings. Each serving has 198 Calories, 8g Fats, 2g Carbohydrates, 29g Protein, and 72mg Cholesterol.

Ingredients:

- ¼ teaspoon of salt
- 1 ¼ lbs. of center cut salmon, slice to make 4 portions
- 2 tablespoons of stone-ground mustard
- ¼ cup of reduced-fat sour cream
- Freshly ground pepper
- 2 teaspoons of lemon juice
- Lemon wedges

Directions:

1. Turn on the broiler. Prepare a baking sheet and line with foil. Grease the foil with cooking spray.

2. Place the salmon fillets with the skin-side facing down on the baking sheet. Season with pepper and salt. Mix together the lemon juice, mustard, and sour cream and spread on top of the salmon.

3. Place the rack 5 inches from heat and bake the salmon for 12 minutes. Serve with the lemon wedges.

11. *Italian Hoagies*

**This recipe makes 4 servings. Each serving has 266 Calories, 8g Fats, 40g Carbohydrates, 14g Protein, and 10mg Cholesterol.

Ingredients:

- 1 (14 oz.) can of artichoke hearts, rinse and chop coarsely
- ¼ cup of thin sliced red onion, separate into rings
- 2 tablespoons of balsamic vinegar
- 1 medium tomato, remove seed and dice
- 1 teaspoon of dried oregano
- 1 tablespoon of extra-virgin olive oil
- 2 slices of provolone cheese, halved
- 1 (20 in) whole grain baguette
- ¼ cup of sliced pepperoncini
- 2 cups of shredded romaine lettuce

Directions:

1. Place the onion rings in a bowl and cover with cold water. Set aside until needed.

2. Mix together the oregano, olive oil, balsamic vinegar, tomato, and

artichoke hearts. Slice the baguette into 4 equal pieces. Split each baguette horizontally.

3. Drain the onions then pat dry.

4. To assemble, divide the provolone among the bottom halves of the baguette. Spread the artichoke mix then top with the onion rings, pepperoncini and lettuce. Place the top halves of the baguette and serve.

12. *Italian Egg Soup*

**This recipe makes 6 servings. Each serving has 266 Calories, 7g Fats, 29g Carbohydrates, 16g Protein, and 128mg Cholesterol.

Ingredients:

- 2 cups of water
- 6 cups of reduced sodium chicken broth
- 1 (7 oz.) can of chickpeas, rinsed
- 1 ⅓ cups of whole wheat medium pasta shells
- A pinch of freshly grated nutmeg
- 1 bunch of scallions, slice then separate the whites and greens
- 4 large eggs, beaten lightly
- 3 cups of chopped arugula, remove tough stems
- 6 tablespoons of freshly grated parmesan cheese
- 2 tablespoons of lemon juice
- Freshly ground pepper

Directions:

1. In a Dutch oven, combine the nutmeg, scallion whites, chickpeas, pasta, water, and chicken broth.

Cover with a lid and set over high heat until boiling. Remove the lid and boil for 5 minutes.

2. Stir in the arugula and cook for a minute. Reduce the heat to low. Stir the soup continuously and slowly add in the eggs. Cook for another 2 minutes. Stir in the lemon juice and scallion greens and season with pepper. Ladle into bowls and top with parmesan before serving.

13. Arugula & Turkey Sausage Pasta

**This recipe makes 6 servings. Each serving has 321 Calories, 8g Fats, 46g Carbohydrates, 19g Protein, and 33mg Cholesterol.

Ingredients:

- 8 oz. of hot Italian turkey sausage, remove from casings
- 12 oz. of whole wheat short pasta
- 8 cups of arugula
- 3 cloves of garlic, chopped
- ½ cup of fine shredded pecorino Romano
- 2 cups of halved cherry tomatoes
- ¼ teaspoon of salt
- 1 teaspoon of freshly ground pepper
- 1 tablespoon of extra-virgin olive oil

Directions:

1. Prepare the pasta according to package directions.

2. In a large skillet, add the sausage and cook over medium-high heat for 5 minutes. Break into smaller pieces. Stir in the tomatoes, arugula

and garlic and cook for another 3 minutes. Remove the skillet from the heat and cover to keep warm.

3. Mix the salt, pepper, and ½ cup of cheese. Reserve ½ cup of the liquid from the pasta before draining the rest. Whisk the oil and cooking liquid into the cheese mix. Add in the pasta and toss until combined. Serve the pasta and top with the sausage mix and cheese.

14. Greek Salad & Sardines

**This recipe makes 4 servings. Each serving has 347 Calories, 18g Fats, 29g Carbohydrates, 7g Protein, and 67mg Cholesterol.

Ingredients:

- 2 tablespoons of extra-virgin olive oil
- 3 tablespoons of lemon juice
- 2 teaspoons of dried oregano
- 1 clove of garlic, mince
- 3 medium tomatoes, cut into chunks
- ½ teaspoon of freshly ground pepper
- 1 (15 oz.) can of chickpeas, rinse
- 1 large English cucumber, cut into chunks
- ¼ cup of thin sliced red onion
- ⅓ cup of crumbled feta cheese
- 2 (4 oz.) cans of sardines in olive oil, drain
- 2 tablespoons of sliced Kalamata olives

Directions:

1. Whisk together the pepper, oregano, garlic, olive oil, and lemon juice.

2. Add in the olives, onion, feta cheese, chickpeas, cucumber, and tomatoes. Toss until well-combined. Top with the sardines and serve.

15. Tomatoes & Roasted Broccoli

**This recipe makes 4 servings. Each serving has 79 Calories, 5g Fats, 8g Carbohydrates, 3g Protein, and 0mg Cholesterol.

Ingredients:

- 1 cup of grape tomatoes
- 12 oz. of broccoli crowns, trim and cut into small florets
- 2 cloves of garlic, mince
- 1 tablespoon of extra-virgin olive oil
- ½ teaspoon of freshly grated lemon zest
- ¼ teaspoon of salt
- 10 pitted black olives, slice
- 1 tablespoon of lemon juice
- 2 teaspoons of capers, rinse
- 1 teaspoon of dried oregano

Directions:

1. Turn on oven and set to 450F.

2. Toss together the salt, garlic, olive oil, tomatoes and broccoli in a large bowl. Spread the mixture in a single layer on top of a baking sheet. Bake for 13 minutes.

3. Mix together the capers, oregano, olives, lemon juice, and lemon zest. Add in the roasted vegetables and stir until well-combined. Serve immediately.

16. Turkey & Onion Quesadillas

**This recipe makes 4 servings. Each serving has Calories, Fats, Carbohydrates, Protein, and Cholesterol.

Ingredients:

- ¼ cup of balsamic vinegar
- 1 small red onion, slice thinly
- 1 cup of shredded sharp cheddar cheese
- 4 (10-in) whole wheat tortillas
- 8 slices of smoked deli turkey

Directions:

1. Combine the balsamic vinegar and red onion in a bowl and marinate for 5 minutes. Drain and reserve the vinegar for future use.

2. Warm each side of the tortillas for 45 seconds in a pan set over medium-high heat. Sprinkle ¼ of the cheddar cheese over each tortilla and place 2 slices of turkey on top. Add ¼ of the onions over each tortilla and fold the tortillas in half.

3. Gently flatten the tortillas with a spatula and cook for 2 minutes. Flip and cook the other side for another 2 minutes. Do the same with the remaining tortillas.

17. Garlic Lemon Shrimp

**This recipe makes 1 serving. Each serving has 82 Calories, 3g Fats, 2g Carbohydrates, 11g Protein, and 100mg Cholesterol.

Ingredients:

- 2 tablespoons of extra-virgin olive oil
- 3 tablespoons of minced garlic
- ¼ cup of minced fresh parsley
- ¼ cup of lemon juice
- ½ teaspoon of pepper
- ½ teaspoon of kosher salt
- 1 ¼ lbs. of cooked shrimp

Directions:

1. Add the oil in a small pan set over medium heat. Add in the garlic and cook for a minute. The next ingredients that you should add are the pepper, salt, parsley, and lemon juice.

2. Place the shrimp in a bowl and pour the mixture on top. Toss together until well-combined and chill until serving time.

18. Pacific Sole

**This recipe makes 2 servings. Each serving has 185 Calories, 9g Fats, 11g Carbohydrates, 16g Protein, and 65mg Cholesterol.

Ingredients:

- 10 oz. of Pacific sole
- 1 orange
- ¼ teaspoon of freshly ground pepper
- ¼ teaspoon of salt
- 1 medium shallot, mince
- 2 teaspoons of unsalted butter
- 2 tablespoons of chopped pecans, toast
- 2 tablespoons of white wine vinegar
- 2 tablespoons of fresh dill

Directions:

1. Remove the skin and pith from the orange using a sharp paring knife. Cut between membranes to take out the orange sections and place it in a bowl together with its juice.

2. Season the Pacific sole with pepper and salt. Grease a nonstick pan

using a cooking spray and set over medium heat. Add in the fillets and cook each side for 1 to 2 minutes. Place on a plate and cover with foil.

3. Add the butter into the same skillet where you cooked the fish and melt over medium heat. Add in the shallots and cook for 30 seconds. Add in the white wine vinegar together with the orange sections and its juice. Cook for 30 seconds loosening any browned bits. Spoon the sauce over the fish and sprinkle the dill and pecans on top before serving.

19. Blueberries & Lemon Cream

**This recipe makes 4 servings. Each serving has 144 Calories, 5g Fats, 21g Carbohydrates, 5g Protein, and 18mg Cholesterol.

Ingredients:

- ¾ cup of vanilla yogurt
- 4 oz. of reduced fat cream cheese
- 2 teaspoons of freshly grated lemon zest
- 1 teaspoon of honey
- 2 cups of fresh blueberries

Directions:

1. Break up the cream cheese in a bowl using a fork. Drain the liquid from the yogurt and add into the bowl. Pour in the honey and mix at high speed using an electric mixer until creamy and light. Stir in the lemon zest.

2. Layer the blueberries and lemon cream on wine glasses and cover. Refrigerate for 8 hours and serve immediately.

20. Roasted Cod with Warm Tapenade

**This recipe makes 4 servings. Each serving has 151 Calories, 8g Fats, 4g Carbohydrates, 15g Protein, and 45mg Cholesterol.

Ingredients:

- 3 teaspoons of extra-virgin olive oil
- 1 lb. of cod fillet
- 1 tablespoon of minced shallot
- ¼ teaspoon of freshly ground pepper
- ¼ cup of chopped cured olives
- 1 cup of halved cherry tomatoes
- 1 ½ teaspoons of chopped fresh oregano
- 1 tablespoon of capers, rinse and chop
- 1 teaspoon of balsamic vinegar

Directions:

1. Turn on the oven and set to 450F. Grease a baking sheet using cooking spray.

2. Rub the cod fillet with 2 teaspoons of the olive oil. Season with pepper.

Place on the baking sheet and bake in the oven for 20 minutes.

3. Heat the remaining olive oil in a small pan set over medium heat. Add in the shallot and cook for 20 seconds. Add in the tomatoes and cook for 12 minutes. Add in the capers and olives and cook for another 30 seconds.

4. Stir in the balsamic vinegar and oregano then remove the pan from the heat. Spoon the sauce over the cod fillet and serve.

21. Shrimp Saltimbocca Over Polenta

**This recipe makes 4 servings. Each serving has 229 Calories, 5g Fats, 20g Carbohydrates, 23g Protein, and 186mg Cholesterol.

Ingredients:

- 1 thin slice of prosciutto
- 1 (18 oz.) tube of polenta, cut to make 8 rounds
- 1 ¼ teaspoons of cornstarch
- 2 tablespoons of lemon juice
- ¼ teaspoon of freshly ground pepper
- 1 lb. of peeled and deveined raw shrimp
- 2 tablespoons of finely diced onion
- 1 tablespoon of extra-virgin olive oil
- 1 tablespoon of chopped fresh sage
- ¾ cup of clam juice

Directions:

1. Place the oven rack at the center and preheat the broiler. Grease a baking sheet using a cooking spray.

2. Arrange the prosciutto and polenta on the baking sheet and broil in the oven for 5 minutes. Transfer the prosciutto on a plate and continue to broil the polenta about 12 minutes on each side.

3. Whisk together the cornstarch and lemon juice. Season the shrimp with ⅛ teaspoon of black pepper. Heat the olive oil in a skillet set over medium heat. Add the onion and cook for 3 minutes. Add shrimp and cook for 2 minutes. Pour in the clam juice then bring to boil. Cook for another 2 minutes.

4. Whisk the cornstarch again and pour into the pan along with the remaining pepper and sage. Cook for 2 minutes while stirring continuously. Place the shrimp and sauce over the polenta and crumble prosciutto on top. Serve immediately.

22. White Bean & Chicken Soup

**This recipe makes 6 servings. Each serving has Calories, Fats, Carbohydrates, Protein, and Cholesterol.

Ingredients:

- 2 leeks, use light green and white parts only and cut into rounds
- 2 teaspoons of extra-virgin olive oil
- 2 (14 oz.) cans of reduced-sodium chicken broth
- 1 tablespoon of chopped fresh sage
- 1 (15 oz.) can of cannellini beans, rinse
- 2 cups of water
- 1 roasted chicken, remove skin and bones then shred

Directions:

1. Heat the olive oil in a Dutch oven set over medium-high heat. Add in the leeks and cook for 3 minutes while stirring often. Stir in the sage and cook for 30 seconds. Stir in the water and chicken broth and adjust the heat to high.

2. Cover with a lid and bring to boil. Add in the beans and chicken and cook uncovered for 3 minutes while stirring occasionally. Serve immediately.

23. Arugula & Italian Sausage Fusilli

**This recipe makes 2 servings. Each serving has 411 Calories, 16g Fats, 48g Carbohydrates, 24g Protein, and 45mg Cholesterol.

Ingredients:

- 4 oz. of hot Italian turkey sausage, remove casing
- 4 oz. of whole wheat fusilli
- 4 cups of arugula
- 2 cloves of garlic, chop
- ¼ cup of fine shredded pecorino Romano
- ½ cup of halved cherry tomatoes
- ⅛ teaspoon of salt
- 1 teaspoon of freshly ground pepper
- 2 teaspoons of extra-virgin olive oil

Directions:

1. Prepare the pasta according to package directions. Reserve 2 tablespoons of the cooking liquid and set the pasta aside until needed.

2. Cook the sausage in a non-stick pan set over medium-high heat for 4

minutes, breaking it into smaller pieces. Stir in the garlic, tomatoes, and arugula and cook for 2 minutes while stirring often. Remove the pan from the heat and cover to keep warm.

3. Combine the salt, pepper, and cheese in a bowl. Whisk in the olive oil and the reserved cooking liquid into the cheese mix and add in the pasta. Toss until well-combined. Top the pasta with the vegetable mixture and serve.

24. Olive Artichoke Tuna Salad

**This recipe makes 5 servings. Each serving has 103 Calories, 5g Fats, 8g Carbohydrates, 8g Protein, and 16mg Cholesterol.

Ingredients:

- 1 cup of chopped canned artichoke hearts
- 1 (12 oz.) can of light chunk tuna, drain and flake
- ⅓ cup of reduced fat mayonnaise
- ½ cup of chopped olives
- 1 ½ teaspoons of chopped fresh oregano
- 2 teaspoons of lemon juice

Directions:

1. Combine all the ingredients in a salad bowl.

2. Serve over salad greens.

Chapter 4 – Mediterranean Dishes for the Vegetarian

1. Parmesan Roasted Cauliflower

**This recipe makes 4 servings. Each serving has 152 Calories, 10g Fats, 10g Carbohydrates, 7g Protein, and 7mg Cholesterol.

Ingredients:

- 2 tablespoons of extra-virgin olive oil
- 8 cups of cauliflower florets
- ¼ teaspoon of salt
- 1 teaspoon of dried marjoram
- 2 tablespoons of balsamic vinegar
- freshly ground pepper
- ½ cup of fine shredded parmesan cheese

Directions:

1. Turn on oven and set to 450F.

2. Toss together the pepper, salt, marjoram, olive oil, and cauliflower. Spread the mixture in a single layer

on a rimmed baking sheet. Roast in the oven for 20 minutes.

3. Toss the cauliflower with balsamic vinegar and sprinkle with parmesan cheese. Roast again for another 10 minutes.

2. Vegetable Ravioli Soup

**This recipe makes 4 servings. Each serving has 261 Calories, 8g Fats, 33g Carbohydrates, 11g Protein, and 28mg Cholesterol.

Ingredients:

- 2 cups of frozen onion and bell pepper mix, thaw and dice
- 1 tablespoon of extra-virgin olive oil
- ¼ teaspoon of crushed red pepper
- 2 cloves of garlic, mince
- 1 (15 oz.) can of vegetable broth
- 1 (28 oz.) can of crushed fire-roasted tomatoes
- 1 teaspoon of dried basil
- 1 ½ cups of hot water
- 2 cups of diced zucchini
- 1 (9 oz.) pack of fresh whole wheat cheese ravioli
- freshly ground pepper

Directions:

1. Heat the olive oil in a Dutch oven set over medium heat. Add in the onion-pepper mix, crushed red pepper, and garlic. Cook for 1 minute while

stirring. Add in the basil, water, vegetable broth, and tomatoes.

2. Increase the heat to high and bring to a boil. Add in the ravioli and cook according to package directions. About 3 minutes left in the cooking time, add in the zucchini to cook. Season before serving.

3. Vegetarian Lasagna

**This recipe makes 8 servings. Each serving has 413 Calories, 14g Fats, 49g Carbohydrates, 27g Protein, and 67mg Cholesterol.

Ingredients:

- 1 (16 oz.) container of part-skim ricotta
- 1 large egg
- 4 small Portobello mushroom caps, remove gills and slice thinly
- 1 (5 oz.) pack of baby spinach, chop coarsely
- 1 (28 oz.) can of crushed tomatoes
- 1 small zucchini, quarter lengthwise and slice thinly
- 3 cloves of garlic, mince
- 1 (28 oz.) can of diced tomatoes
- 15 whole wheat lasagna noodles, uncooked
- a pinch of crushed red pepper
- 3 cups of shredded part-skim mozzarella

Directions:

1. Mix together the zucchini, mushrooms, spinach, ricotta, and egg in a bowl.

2. In another bowl, mix the crushed red pepper, garlic, diced tomatoes, and crushed tomatoes.

3. Grease a slow cooker with cooking spray and cover the bottom with 1 ½ cups of the tomato sauce. Place 5 noodles over the sauce and spread half of the ricotta mixture on top of the noodles. Pat down firmly and spoon 1 ½ cups of sauce on top. Cover with 1 cup of the mozzarella and repeat the layering again beginning with the noodles. Set aside the remaining mozzarella until the lasagna is cooked.

4. Cover the slow cooker with its lid and set to high. Cook for 2 hours and sprinkle the reserved mozzarella on top of the lasagna. Replace the lid and let stand for 10 minutes or until the cheese has melted.

4. Eggplant Pomodoro

**This recipe makes 6 servings. Each serving has 283 Calories, 7g Fats, 50g Carbohydrates, 10g Protein, and omg Cholesterol.

Ingredients:

- 1 medium eggplant, cut into cubes
- 2 tablespoons of extra-virgin olive oil
- 4 plum tomatoes, dice
- 2 cloves of garlic, mince
- 2 tablespoons of red wine vinegar
- ⅓ cup of chopped pitted green olives
- ¾ teaspoon of salt
- 4 teaspoon of capers, rinse
- ¼ teaspoon of crushed red pepper
- ½ teaspoon of freshly ground pepper
- ¼ cup of chopped fresh basil
- 12 oz. of whole wheat angel hair pasta

Directions:

1. Prepare the pasta according to package directions. Set aside and prepare the sauce.

2. Set a large skillet over medium heat and add in the olive oil. Once hot, add in the eggplant and cook for 5 minutes while stirring occasionally. Add the garlic and cook for another minute. Add in the crushed red pepper, pepper, salt, capers, red wine vinegar, olives, and tomatoes. Cook for 7 minutes while stirring continuously.

3. Place the pasta on a serving dish and pour the sauce on top. Sprinkle basil on top and serve.

5. Butter Beans & Sautéed Polenta

**This recipe makes 4 servings. Each serving has 221 Calories, 9g Fats, 28g Carbohydrates, 10g Protein, and 13mg Cholesterol.

Ingredients:

- 1 (16 oz.) tube of prepared plain polenta, cut into cubes
- 4 teaspoons of extra-virgin olive oil
- 1 small onion, slice thinly
- 1 clove of garlic, mince
- ½ teaspoon of smoked paprika
- 1 red bell pepper, dice
- 4 cups of packed baby spinach
- 1 (15 oz.) can of butter beans, rinse
- ½ cup of shredded manchego
- ¾ cup of vegetable broth
- 2 teaspoons of sherry vinegar

Directions:

1. Add 2 teaspoons of olive oil in a large pan set over medium-high heat. Add in the polenta and cook for 10 minutes while stirring occasionally. Once done, transfer the polenta into a plate.

2. Adjust the heat to medium and add the remaining olive oil. Once the oil is hot, add in the garlic and cook for 30 seconds. Add the bell pepper and onion and cook for 5 minutes while stirring continuously. Add the paprika and cook for 30 seconds.

3. Stir in the vegetable broth, spinach and beans. Cook for 3 minutes while stirring continuously. Remove the pan from the heat and stir in the sherry vinegar and cheese. Top each polenta with the vegetables and sprinkle with more paprika to serve.

6. Mushroom Fettuccine

**This recipe makes 4 servings. Each serving has 314 Calories, 11g Fats, 47g Carbohydrates, 12g Protein, and 9mg Cholesterol.

Ingredients:

- 3 cloves of garlic, mince
- 2 tablespoons of extra-virgin olive oil
- 2 teaspoons of freshly grated lemon zest
- 2 oz. of shiitake mushrooms, remove the stems and slice
- ¼ teaspoon of salt
- 2 tablespoons of lemon juice
- 8 oz. of whole wheat fettuccine
- Freshly ground pepper
- ½ cup of freshly grated parmesan cheese
- ½ cup of chopped fresh basil

Directions:

1. Prepare the pasta according to package directions and reserve ½ cup of the cooking liquid.

2. In a large pan set over low heat, add in the olive oil. Once hot, add in the garlic and cook for 1 minute while stirring continuously. Add in the mushrooms and adjust the heat to medium-high. Cook for 5 minutes. Stir in the pepper, salt, lemon juice, and lemon zest. Remove the pan from the heat.

3. Add the reserved cooking liquid, pasta, ¼ cup of basil, and the parmesan cheese into the pan and toss until well-combined. Serve immediately and top with the remaining basil.

7. Bean Bolognese

**This recipe makes 4 servings. Each serving has 442 Calories, 11g Fats, 68g Carbohydrates, 18g Protein, and 9mg Cholesterol.

Ingredients:

- 2 tablespoons of extra-virgin olive oil
- 1 (14 oz.) can of salad beans, rinse
- ½ cup of chopped carrot
- 1 small onion, chop
- ½ teaspoon of salt
- ¼ cup of chopped celery
- 1 bay leaf
- 4 cloves of garlic, chop
- 1 (14 oz.) can of diced tomatoes
- ½ cup of white wine
- 8 oz. of whole wheat fettuccine
- ¼ cup of chopped fresh parsley
- ½ cup of freshly grated parmesan cheese

Directions:

1. Prepare the pasta according to package directions. Set aside until needed.

2. Mash ½ cup of beans with a fork.

3. Heat the olive oil in a saucepan set over medium heat. Add in the celery, salt, carrot, and onion and cook for 10 minutes while stirring continuously. Add the bay leaf and garlic and cook for 15 seconds. Add the white wine and adjust the heat to high. Boil for 4 minutes.

4. Stir in the tomatoes, mashed beans, and 2 tablespoons of parsley. Simmer and cook for 6 minutes while stirring occasionally. Add the remaining beans and cook for another 2 minutes.

5. Place the pasta into a serving platter. Discard the bay leaf and pour the sauce over the pasta. Sprinkle with the remaining parsley and parmesan cheese.

8. Eggplant Parmesan

**This recipe makes 6 servings. Each serving has 204 Calories, 6g Fats, 29g Carbohydrates, 11g Protein, and 13mg Cholesterol.

Ingredients:

- 3 egg whites
- 2 eggplants
- 1 cup of fine dry breadcrumbs
- 3 tablespoons of water
- ½ teaspoon of salt
- ½ cup of freshly grated parmesan cheese
- ¼ cup of slivered fresh basil leaves
- ½ teaspoon of freshly ground pepper
- ¾ cup of grated part-skim mozzarella cheese
- 2 ½ cups of tomato sauce

Directions:

1. Turn on oven and set to 400F. Grease two baking sheets and an 8-inch baking dish with cooking spray.

2. Slice the eggplants crosswise to make ¼-in thick pieces. Whisk the

water and egg whites until frothy. Mix together the breadcrumbs, pepper, salt, and ¼ cup of the parmesan cheese. Dip the eggplant pieces into the egg white mix then coat with the breadcrumb mix. Arrange the eggplants on the baking sheets and bake for 15 minutes.

3. Mix together the tomato sauce and basil. Spread ½ cup of the mixture into the bottom of the baking dish. Arrange the eggplant slices in a single layer on top of the sauce. Spoon 1 cup of the tomato sauce over the eggplants and sprinkle ½ of the mozzarella cheese. Add another layer of eggplant slices and top with the remaining sauce and cheese. Bake in the oven for 20 minutes.

9. Whole Wheat Pizza

**This recipe makes 6 servings. Each serving has 765 Calories, 13g Fats, 141g Carbohydrates, 25g Protein, and omg Cholesterol.

Ingredients:

For the dough

- ¾ cup of all-purpose flour
- ¾ cup of whole wheat flour
- ¾ teaspoon of salt
- 1 pack of quick rising yeast
- ⅔ cup of hot water
- ¼ teaspoon of sugar
- 2 teaspoons of extra-virgin olive oil

Directions:

1. In a food processor, add the sugar, salt, yeast, all-purpose flour, and whole wheat flour. Pulse to combine. Mix together the oil and hot water and gradually pour in the liquid into the food processor until the mixture forms a soft, sticky ball. Process for another minute.

2. Transfer the dough into a flat and lightly floured surface. Grease a sheet of plastic wrap using a cooking spray and place it over the dough with the sprayed-side sticking to the dough. Rest for 20 minutes.

3. Place a pizza stone on the lowest rack in the oven.

4. Turn on oven and set to 500F. Roll and top the pizza according to preference and bake in the oven for 14 minutes. Serve immediately.

10. Black Bean & Smoky Corn Pizza

**This recipe makes 6 servings. Each serving has 302 Calories, 9g Fats, 48g Carbohydrates, 13g Protein, and 15mg Cholesterol.

Ingredients:

- 1 cup of canned black beans, rinse
- 1 plum tomato, dice
- 2 tablespoons of cornmeal
- 1 cup of fresh corn kernels
- ⅓ cup of barbecue sauce
- 1 lb. of prepared whole wheat pizza dough
- 1 cup of shredded smoked mozzarella

Directions:

1. Turn on grill and set to medium heat.

2. Mix together the corn, beans, and tomato in a bowl. Scatter the cornmeal on a baking sheet. Stretch the dough to make a 12-inch circle and place it over the cornmeal covering its entire underside.

3. Transfer the crust to the grill and close the lid. Cook for 5 minutes.

4. Flip the crust using a spatula and spread barbecue sauce on top. Sprinkle the tomato mix and the cheese on top. Close the lid again and grill for 5 minutes.

11. *Broccoli Corn Calzones*

**This recipe makes 6 servings. Each serving has 348 Calories, 12g Fats, 49g Carbohydrates, 17g Protein, and 21mg Cholesterol.

Ingredients:

- 1 ½ cups of fresh corn kernels
- 1 ½ cups of chopped broccoli florets
- ⅔ cup of part-skim ricotta cheese
- 1 cup of shredded part-skim mozzarella cheese
- ¼ cup of chopped fresh basil
- 4 scallions, sliced thinly
- ¼ teaspoon of salt
- ½ teaspoon of garlic powder
- all-purpose flour
- ¼ teaspoon of freshly ground pepper
- 2 teaspoons of canola oil
- 20 oz. of prepared whole wheat pizza dough

Directions:

1. Place the racks in the upper third and lower third of the oven. Turn on the heat and set to 475F. Grease the baking sheets with cooking spray.

2. Mix pepper, salt, garlic powder, basil, scallions, ricotta cheese, mozzarella cheese, corn, and broccoli.

3. Divide the dough into 6 equal parts and place on a flat, lightly-floured surface. Roll each piece to make an 8-inch circle. Place ¾ cup of the vegetable mixture on ½ of each circle leaving about 1 inch of border. Brush the border with water and fold the half over the filling. Crimp the edges using a fork to seal. Make small slits on the top part to create a vent. Brush with oil and transfer the calzones on the baking sheets.

4. Bake the calzones 7 minutes on top rack and 8 minutes on the bottom rack. Cool slightly before serving.

12. Cheesy Polenta and Roasted Winter Vegetables

**This recipe makes 4 servings. Each serving has 329 Calories, 14g Fats, 43g Carbohydrates, 14g Protein, and 20mg Cholesterol.

Ingredients:

- 4 cups of cubed and peeled butternut squash
- 4 cups of cauliflower florets
- 2 tablespoons of extra-virgin olive oil
- 1 medium onion, sliced
- ¾ teaspoon of freshly ground pepper
- ½ teaspoon of garlic powder
- 2 ½ cups of vegetable broth
- ¼ teaspoon of salt
- ¾ cup of cornmeal
- 1 cup of water
- ⅔ cup of fine shredded parmesan cheese
- 1 teaspoon of chopped fresh rosemary

Directions:

1. Turn on oven and set to 500F.

2. Toss the salt ½ teaspoon of pepper, garlic powder, olive oil, onion, squash, and cauliflower. Spread the vegetables on a rimmed baking sheet. Roast in the oven for 30 minutes.

3. Combine the water and vegetable broth in a saucepan and bring to boil. Whisk in the remaining pepper, rosemary, and cornmeal. Reset the heat to low and cover the saucepan with a lid. Cook for 15 minutes while stirring occasionally. Stir in the cheese then remove the saucepan from the heat. Serve the vegetables over the polenta.

13. Zucchini & Tortellini Soup

**This recipe makes 6 servings. Each serving has 198 Calories, 8g Fats, 27g Carbohydrates, 7g Protein, and 10mg Cholesterol.

Ingredients:

- 2 large carrots, chop finely
- 2 tablespoons of extra-virgin olive oil
- 2 tablespoons of minced garlic
- 1 large onion, diced
- 2 (14 oz.) cans of vegetable broth
- 1 teaspoon of chopped fresh rosemary
- 9 oz. of fresh spinach cheese tortellini
- 2 medium zucchini, diced
- 2 tablespoons of red wine vinegar
- 4 plum tomatoes, diced

Directions:

1. Heat the olive oil in a Dutch oven set over medium heat. Add in the onion and carrots. Cover with a lid and cook for 7 minutes while stirring occasionally. Stir in the rosemary and garlic. Cook for 1 minute.

2. Stir in the zucchini and the vegetable broth. Bring to boil. Reduce the heat and simmer for 3 minutes while stirring occasionally. Add the tomatoes and tortellini and simmer for another 10 minutes. Stir in the vinegar just before serving.

14. Lemon Asparagus Pasta

**This recipe makes 2 servings. Each serving has 395 Calories, 12g Fats, 56g Carbohydrates, 19g Protein, and 26mg Cholesterol.

Ingredients:

- ½ bunch of asparagus, trim and cut to ¾-inch pieces
- 4 oz. of whole wheat penne
- 2 teaspoons of whole grain mustard
- ¾ cup of whole milk
- ⅛ teaspoon of salt
- 2 teaspoons of all-purpose flour
- 1 teaspoon of extra-virgin olive oil
- ¼ teaspoon of freshly ground pepper
- 1 teaspoon of minced fresh tarragon
- 2 tablespoons of minced garlic
- 1 teaspoon of lemon juice
- ¼ teaspoon of freshly grated lemon zest
- ½ cup of freshly grated parmesan cheese

Directions:

1. Fill a large saucepan with water and bring to boil. Add the pasta and cook

for 6 minutes. Add in the asparagus and continue cooking for another 3 minutes while stirring occasionally. Drain the water and return the pasta and asparagus into the saucepan.

2. Whisk together the pepper, salt, flour, mustard, and milk in a bowl. Heat the olive oil in a small saucepan set over medium-high heat. Add in the garlic and cook for 1 minute while stirring constantly. Stir in the milk mixture. Bring to simmer and cook for 2 minutes while stirring constantly. Stir in the lemon juice, lemon zest, and tarragon.

3. Mix together the cooked pasta and the sauce and place the pan saucepan over medium-high heat. Cook until the sauce becomes thick and creamy while stirring constantly. Stir in ¼ cup of parmesan and mix until combined. Top with the remaining cheese and serve.

15. Chickpea & Eggplant Stew

**This recipe makes 8 servings. Each serving has 220 Calories, 7g Fats, 33g Carbohydrates, 9g Protein, and 0mg Cholesterol.

Ingredients:

- 3 cups of hot water
- 1 oz. of dried porcini mushrooms
- 3 tablespoons of extra-virgin olive oil
- 2 large eggplants
- 6 cloves of garlic, minced
- 2 large onions, sliced thinly
- 1 small cinnamon stick
- 2 teaspoons of dried oregano, crumble
- 1 teaspoon of freshly ground pepper
- 1 teaspoon of salt
- 1 cup of dried chickpeas, rinse and soak overnight then drain
- 1 bay leaf
- ¼ cup of fine chopped fresh parsley
- 1 (28 oz.) can of tomatoes, drain and chop coarsely

Directions:

1. Turn on oven and set to 400F.

2. Combine the hot water and mushrooms in a bowl. Mix well and let stand for ½ hour. Strain using a sieve lined with a sheet of paper towel and reserve the liquid. Chop the mushrooms finely.

3. Cut the eggplants in half lengthwise and brush the cut sides with 2 tablespoons of oil. Place the eggplants on a rimmed baking sheet with the cut side facing down. Roast for 25 minutes and set aside to cool slightly. Cut to make 1-inch cubes and add to the slow cooker.

4. Heat the remaining olive oil in a large pan set over medium heat. Add in the onions and cook for 6 minutes while stirring frequently. Add the mushrooms, bay leaf, pepper, salt, cinnamon stick, oregano, and garlic. Stir and cook for 1 minute. Add in the chickpeas and the reserved liquid and bring to boil. Cook for 5 minutes while stirring occasionally. Transfer the

contents to the slow cooker and mix with the eggplant.

5. Cover with the lid and cook for 4 hours over high settings. To serve, remove the bay leaf and cinnamon stick and stir in the parsley and tomatoes.

16. Barley & Butternut Pilaf

**This recipe makes 6 servings. Each serving has 175 Calories, 2g Fats, 36g Carbohydrates, 5g Protein, and 0mg Cholesterol.

Ingredients:

- 1 medium onion, chop
- 2 teaspoons of extra-virgin olive oil
- 1 ¾ cups of water
- 1 (14 oz.) can of reduced-sodium chicken broth
- 2 cups of peeled and cubed butternut squash
- 1 cup of pearl barley
- 1 teaspoon of freshly grated lemon zest
- ⅓ cup of chopped flat-leaf parsley
- 1 clove of garlic, mince
- 1 tablespoon of lemon juice
- Freshly ground pepper
- ¼ teaspoon of salt

Directions:

1. Heat the olive oil in a large pan set over medium heat. Add in the onion and cook for 3 minutes while stirring often. Add in the squash, barley,

water, and chicken broth into the pan and bring to simmer.

2. Reduce the heat to medium-low and cook the squash for 45 minutes. Stir in the pepper, salt, garlic, lemon juice, lemon zest, and parsley.

17. Vegetable Polenta Bake

**This recipe makes 8 servings. Each serving has 201 Calories, 9g Fats, 23g Carbohydrates, 9g Protein, and 14mg Cholesterol.

Ingredients:

- 1 medium eggplant, dice
- 2 tablespoons of extra-virgin olive oil
- ½ teaspoon of salt
- 1 small zucchini, finely dice
- ½ cup of water
- ½ teaspoon of freshly ground pepper
- 1 ½ cups of prepared marinara sauce
- 10 oz. of baby spinach
- 14 oz. of prepared polenta, slice lengthwise to make 6 thin slices
- ½ cup of chopped fresh basil
- 1 ½ cups of shredded part-skim mozzarella

Directions:

1. Turn on oven and set to 450F. Grease a 9-inch baking dish using cooking spray.

2. Heat the olive oil in a large pan set over medium-high heat. Add in the salt pepper, zucchini, and eggplant and cook for 6 minutes while stirring occasionally. Add in the spinach and water and cook for 3 minutes stirring once. Stir in the marinara sauce and cook for another 2 minutes. Remove the pan from the heat and stir in the basil.

3. Arrange the polenta slices in one layer in the baking dish. Sprinkle ¾ cup of cheese and Spread the vegetable mixture on top. Cover with the remaining cheese. Bake in the oven for 15 minutes. Cool for 5 minutes before serving.

18. Chickpea Nuts

**This recipe makes 4 servings. Each serving has 131 Calories, 5g Fats, 19g Carbohydrates, 4g Protein, and 0mg Cholesterol.

Ingredients:

- 1 tablespoon of extra-virgin olive oil
- 1 (15 oz.) can of chickpeas, rinse
- 1 teaspoon of dried marjoram
- 2 teaspoons of ground cumin
- ¼ teaspoon of salt
- ¼ teaspoon of ground allspice

Directions:

1. Place the rack in the upper third of the oven and turn it on. Set to 450F.

2. Pat dry the chickpeas and toss together with the salt, allspice, marjoram, cumin, and olive oil in a bow. Spread in a single layer on a baking sheet with rim. Bake in the oven for 30 minutes stirring once. Cool for 15 minutes before serving.

19. *Almond Lentil Burger*

**This recipe makes 5 servings. Each serving has 236 Calories, 9g Fats, 28g Carbohydrates, 12g Protein, and 27mg Cholesterol.

Ingredients:

- 1 cup of brown lentils
- 6 cups of water
- ¾ cup of fine chopped carrot
- 2 tablespoons of extra-virgin olive oil
- ⅓ cup of fine chopped celery
- ⅓ cup of fine chopped shallots
- 1 teaspoon of chopped fresh thyme
- ¼ cup of sliced almonds
- ¼ teaspoon of freshly ground pepper
- ½ teaspoon of salt
- 1 tablespoon of lemon juice
- 1 large egg yolk, beaten lightly

Directions:

1. Fill a large saucepan with water and bring to a boil. Add in the lentils and adjust the heat to medium-low. Simmer for 25 minutes. Drain through a fine mesh sieve.

2. Heat 1 tablespoon of olive oil in a large pans set over medium heat. Add in the celery, shallots, and carrot and cook for 3 minutes while stirring continuously. Stir in the salt, pepper, thyme, and almonds and cook for another 2 minutes. Transfer the mixture in a food processor and add in 1 cup of the lentils.

3. Pulse for a few times until the mixture is coarsely ground. Transfer to a mixing bowl and mix in the remaining lentils. Cool for 10 minutes. Mix in the lemon juice and egg yolk and cover. Refrigerate for an hour.

4. Form the lentil mix into 5 patties. Heat the remaining olive oil in a large pan set over medium-high heat. Add in the patties and cook each side for 4 minutes. Serve immediately.

20. Fassoulatha

**This recipe makes 8 servings. Each serving has 256 Calories, 5g Fats, 42g Carbohydrates, 13g Protein, and 0mg Cholesterol.

Ingredients:

- 2 tablespoons of extra-virgin olive oil
- 1 lb. of dried white beans, soak overnight
- 2 stalks of celery, chop finely
- 2 large onions, chop finely
- 1 quart of water
- 2 large carrots, chop finely
- 2 teaspoons of dried oregano
- 2 large ripe tomatoes, peel and mash
- ⅛ teaspoon of cayenne pepper
- 1 teaspoon of salt
- freshly ground pepper

Directions:

1. Fill a large pot with water and bring to boil. Drain the beans and add into the pot. Cover the pot with a lid and cook for 1 ½ hours. Drain and set the beans aside until needed.

2. Heat the olive oil in a soup pot set over medium heat. Sauté the carrots, celery, and onions for 5 minutes. Add in the pepper, cayenne, salt, oregano, tomatoes, and beans into the pot. Mix then simmer for 20 minutes. Taste and add more seasoning as necessary.

Conclusion

I hope you have learned a lot from this book and enjoyed the recipes as much as I did. Now that you have learned the basic principles, you can also create your own Mediterranean recipes. I hope that this book helped you reach your goals.
If you have enjoyed this book, please leave a review for the book.
Thanks again for reading this book and good luck!

Check out more books by Celine Walker!

7145R00157

Printed in Great Britain
by Amazon